THIS IS IT!

God is Love!

[signature]

THIS IS IT!

The Ultimate Handbook for Successful Living

Dr. Stan Gravely, PhD

Copyright © 2013 Dr. Stan Gravely, PhD.

All rights reserved. No part of this book may be used or reproduced by any means, graphic, electronic, or mechanical, including photocopying, recording, taping or by any information storage retrieval system without the written permission of the publisher except in the case of brief quotations embodied in critical articles and reviews.

Balboa Press books may be ordered through booksellers or by contacting:

Balboa Press
A Division of Hay House
1663 Liberty Drive
Bloomington, IN 47403
www.balboapress.com
1-(877) 407-4847

Because of the dynamic nature of the Internet, any web addresses or links contained in this book may have changed since publication and may no longer be valid. The views expressed in this work are solely those of the author and do not necessarily reflect the views of the publisher, and the publisher hereby disclaims any responsibility for them.

The author of this book does not dispense medical advice or prescribe the use of any technique as a form of treatment for physical, emotional, or medical problems without the advice of a physician, either directly or indirectly. The intent of the author is only to offer information of a general nature to help you in your quest for emotional and spiritual well-being. In the event you use any of the information in this book for yourself, which is your constitutional right, the author and the publisher assume no responsibility for your actions.

Any people depicted in stock imagery provided by Thinkstock are models, and such images are being used for illustrative purposes only.
Certain stock imagery © Thinkstock.

Printed in the United States of America

ISBN: 978-1-4525-6856-0 (sc)
ISBN: 978-1-4525-6858-4 (hc)
ISBN: 978-1-4525-6857-7 (e)

Library of Congress Control Number: 2013902545

Balboa Press rev. date: 2/25/2013

What You Conceive in your Mind, have Faith in, and Confess, will Manifest!

Table of Contents

The is IT! . . . . *ix*
Chapter 1   Spiritual Life 1
Spiritual Affirmations 21
Chapter 2   Mental Life 27
Chapter 3   Family Life 41
Chapter 4   Physical Life 53
Chapter 5   Financial Life 77
Chapter 6   Social Life 87
Chapter 7   The Science of Life 95
Chapter 8   What the Hell? 107
Chapter 9   Conclusion 115
Biographical *117*

THE IS IT!

THE ULTIMATE HANDBOOK FOR SUCCESS

YOU, like most people, are born with a desire to live a successful life in every way possible. It is only natural that people want to have a life filled with purpose, hope, and meaning while experiencing love, joy, peace, contentment and success in every area. When we are born into this world we are filled with wonder and curiosity about life. We are born with vivid imaginations that cause us to dream and imagine wonderful things. We believe that dreams can come true and that we can live an awesome life filled with fun and adventure. Yes, we were born to live a magnificent life and use our imaginations to grow, expand, create, and live life to its fullest extent. No one is born into this world that does not have the potential to live a happy, successful life! IT is our birthright and IT is available to all who become aware of this truth.

This Handbook teaches an art and science of living a life of beauty, happiness, love, peace, joy, contentment, goodness, and vibrancy in every area of life. The art and science of living seeks to develop all sides of our life, nature, and being. This handbook is written to encourage you to live a successful life and assist you to grow and expand in every way. If you seem to be in a rut, then this handbook will assist YOU to overcome whatever obstacles may be hindering you from living an awesome life. Everyone, including YOU

We are all spiritual beings put here on Earth to evolve, grow, expand, and reach our full potential. IT is exciting to know that we can set our intentions to succeed and create a wonderful life! IT is your destiny. IT is your right. As nature expresses the beauty of the universe, so as humans we are endowed with the creative urge to express the Infinite Intelligence of God and the Universe. This irresistible urge pushes everything in life to move forward, expand, grow and reflect the beauty of Its Creator. The Creator has been called many things such as God, Infinite Intelligence, Spirit, Light, and a whole host of names. Whatever you call God, realize that God is the Divine Intelligence of the Universe who has willed and programmed all of creation to grow, expand and reflect the beauty of life. We are created to express God in every aspect of our lives. When we come to realize this fact, we ignite the creative power of the universe within us to rule and take dominion over all of life. IT enables us to be empowered, enlightened, and energized to live a successful life.

IT is the eternal mandate of nature and the laws of the universe that all of life is seeking to express ITS life in some way. We are indeed spiritual beings put here to evolve and expand the beauty of God and the universe. We were created to reflect the image of God, and co-create as God. We are created to take charge of our life, take dominion over life, and reflect the character of God in all we say and do. There is within us the urge to be co-creators with God and to experience the beauty of life. Your spirit energy came from God and is always seeking an outlet or a way to express God, expand God, and co-create with God. This divine spark is a powerful urge that drives us all to live a successful life filled with health, wealth, happiness and success. **IT is your destiny!**

Now is the time to begin your journey to success! **IT is your time!** This handbook's purpose is to help you awaken to the laws of God and the

Universe so that you can be empowered to live your life to **ITS** fullest extent. You are a special and wonderful person who has been put here to live and expand. No hindrance and no obstacle can hold you back but yourself! YOU are full of great potential! Yes, there is so much more to know and understand, but you can learn to succeed! Success requires transformation and change. The process is not for the weak, fearful, or cowards of real change. Challenge yourself! Be open, observant, and receptive, but don't be gullible! Embrace your true self by expanding your reality to go beyond your present understandings. Make a choice that you can change, develop, expand, grow, and be successful in every way.

We have all been conditioned by environmental factors such as family, friends, race, creeds, education, religion, politics, economics, and a variety of philosophies. These influences can be powerful strongholds of belief that can hold you back, keep you unaware, and keep you shackled to earthly ties. When you allow others to think for you and/or succumb to the social pressure of these influences, you become a drifter who allows others to shape your life. If you are not in control of your life, then you are at the mercy of others. The majority of people allow environmental factors to control, manipulate, and dominate their lives. They live in invisible prisons and are the by-products of those they have allowed to affect their belief systems. But YOU do not have to be controlled by the tyranny of these environmental influences. YOU have the power to break these soul ties and embrace expansion, growth, and change!

Challenge yourself but be open and observant, and again don't be gullible. Expand your horizons by expanding your perceptions. Challenging your old feelings, beliefs, and convictions about life is not easy! You will feel pressure from well meaning parents, friends, preachers, teachers, politicians, and ultimately the world. It never fails, when you begin to challenge social systems of belief, many will feel threatened, offended, and/or sincerely concerned and worried over your new choices. As we challenge ourselves, we ultimately challenge those around us. To expand, grow, and lift ourselves up to new levels requires determination and willingness to escape the prison of conditioning. What we perceive and how we interpret our perceptions affects who we are, where we are, what we do, when we do things, and how we do things. The sum total of our life is based on these factors. We are where we are in life based on how we have processed everything up to this point. You are 100% totally responsible for who you are right now and you are 100% able to change that if you like! This is the first step to living a new and better life. YOU make a choice to change. YOU decide to wake up and reset your reference points from the experiences that have formed you up to this point and say YES to expansion, growth, and change!

The first step in success is waking up and awakening to what life truly is. In this step we are re-setting our reference points of seeing and perceiving ourselves and the world we live in. When people are born into this world, they begin to be conditioned by many environmental factors. It is only natural for us to be influenced by our parents, family, religion, schools, peers, friends, books, magazines, and all the other environmental factors that shape our beliefs and interpretations of life. Reality is more often the result of perceptions and interpretations of our environmental influences. This is why nothing is absolute in the mind of man as we are always changing and sometimes struggling with truth. This sets the stage for conflict within and conflict with others.

This is why many times we will settle for a perceived absolute truth that can direct our lives based on religion, science, philosophical systems and social networks we grew up with. This is only natural for most people to settle for and adhere to environmental and social influences rather than to challenge them. People are comfortable with sticking with the crowd and agreeing with religious people that their scriptures are the final say so, or the facts of science are the final say so, or whatever else you are willing to submit your belief system to. **This is why we see so much conflict in the world today.** Everyone has surrendered to some form of truth they are comfortable with and we assume that we are right and everybody else is wrong. After all, if we did not think we were right, we would have to admit to being wrong! And if we are right, then everybody should believe like we do!

When we begin to awaken from this need to have some absolute system to guide our lives, we realize that we can re-set our reference points and escape the prisons of conditioning. As we escape from these self-imposed invisible prisons we can break out and truly live! We can now make life-affirming choices and make way for true transformation and change. You can change! You can break free from and expand your awareness! As we become open and observing, we can broaden and expand our horizons. This does not mean we become gullible and foolish, but it does allow the universe to expand around us and send us new information. One way to do this is to learn to be an observer and an eye witness of your experiences. When we observe we break the barriers of time, the pain of the moment, the agony of defeat, and even the lust of power. When we realize that life is more than just good and bad, we break through to real living. We realize we are more than our circumstances. We realize life is more than just being happy or sad with the way things are or are not. We realize that who we are is more than where we are in the physical situations of life.

It is here that **we awaken** to our spiritual self which is our true self. At this point we awaken to the fact that we are spirit and that we are here experiencing this world in a physical body that is not our true self. When we stop allowing our physical bodies to rule our spirit, and we chose to allow our true self to rule our bodies, we are set free! Yes, life can have its ups and downs in this process of becoming aware, but as we work through being attached to our physical life and learn how to identify with our spiritual self, we will expand and grow. As most religions teach that God is Spirit, so are we! We are spirit, we are spiritual energy. We are more than a physical body! We are a network of energy and intelligence that is in a constant state of communication within ourselves and outside ourselves. We are interconnected with God and the universe and we need to realize that we are extensions of God and the universe. When we awaken to this truth we can now learn how to live in harmony with the universe and live a life of love, joy, peace, and contentment as we continue to grow and expand. As we harmonize with life, we awaken to new and exciting truths. Truth will find you if you allow the universe to bring it to you! So wipe the slate clean and ask the universe to open up to you! When you do, the world will conspire to send you the tools, the resources, and the people you need to succeed and expand your horizons.

Are you awake yet? I hope you are waking up and realizing who you really are! That is why the next step to becoming successful is to learn some basic principles that we need to flow with. As we come to realize we are more than physical beings, we can now begin to reprogram and reset the energy fields of our lives. That is why we have to awaken to the principles and laws of the universe that are immutable, predictable, and available to everyone! They are principles that are absolute truth and will never let you down. That's how we know the truth! The truth never fails and never changes! It is a constant and neutral power that can be relied on and trusted in without fail. In this we can be confident!

Principle One: Believe in Success! Make a conscious decision right now that you want to be successful and experience life as it was meant to be. Belief in this principle is having the confidence and faith to move beyond where you are. Faith and belief in yourself, your life, and your abilities is paramount to living the successful life that allows you to experience the love, joy, peace and contentment of fulfilling your destiny. You were not born into this world to settle for less. IT is your birth right to succeed! So believe it and receive it!

Principle Two: Be a Visionary! If you do not have a vision or a dream then you will perish in defeat. Ask God and the universe to show you who you really are. What are your talents and gifts? What are your desires? What do you really want to do and accomplish? Write down the visions, the dreams and desires of your heart and activate a plan to activate the process of achieving your goals. Remember, what we say and how we say things affects who we are and where we are in life. What you speak is what you get! The tongue speaks and the body listens. Don't be hung by the tongue! What we envision and what we say affects who we are and where we are going. Know who you are and who you are becoming. Write it down, speak it and have supreme faith that IT is so and IT will be!

Principle Three: Burn with Desire! Develop a burning desire to fulfill the dreams and visions you have for life. Develop a dogged determination to follow through with your visions and never give up! Whatever you ardently desire, imagine, believe and act on with the faith and zeal of a crusader will inevitably come to pass. Remain steadfast, unmovable, and always remain persistent. Keep your eyes fixed on what is before you and don't accept fear, doubt, lack or defeat. Be excited and happy about your life and the vision that is unfolding before your eyes! A joyful life radiates with the power of the universe and is like a good medicine that heals and restores health. Stop being negative and be positive!

Principle Four: Be Pro-Active! Develop a plan and take action! It is easier to guide a ship when it is in motion than when it is sitting still. A wise man will count the cost, get organized and have a plan of action. Begin with the end in mind. Adjust and be flexible when necessary but always remember the vision stays constant.

Principle Five: Be Yourself! You are awesome and special. You have intellect, wisdom, creativity, imagination, reason and talent programmed into your very essence. Live your life and refuse to live someone else's life. Take the pressure off yourself and embrace your true self, not one imposed on you by others. I believe that God is love and that when we awaken to this truth we can love ourselves and others in a healthy way. The love of the God builds up and encourages us always no matter who we are or where we are in our life. Love is patient, kind, gentle and never gives up on anyone! Be happy with the person you are and recognize in yourself where you need to improve and take action to better yourself. Not because someone has laid a guilt trip on you, but because you desire to expand and grow into true success.

So let the journey begin! Take responsibility now for your life. Direct your thoughts control your emotions and you will ordain your destiny! God and the universe conspire only to support you and assist you to live a successful life. Stop believing in the lies that hold you back and start living the life YOU are ordained to live! IT is time to make over your life and create a new life of true success and prosperity in every area of life! **It is YOUR time!**

Chapter One

Spiritual Life

We are spiritual beings experiencing life in a biological body here on planet earth. We are spiritual energy and that energy has its beginnings in the absolute energy of the universe we call GOD. God is Light, God is Energy, and God is Love. God is Spirit and those who know God know him by the Spirit. Religion has attempted to define God and teach about God in a myriad of ways but seldom do people ever find the truth that sets them free in religion. Religion for the most part teaches that we are all flawed people in need of salvation through some means of religious codes, doctrines, rituals, formulas and systems. Religion has failed to help people overcome their 'worthiness issues' because religion reminds them all the time that they are sinners and dirty rotten scumbags that need redemption. As a Jew, Muslim or Christian, you are taught that you are all born as a sinner and are destined to go to hell unless you go through some religious prescription for salvation. As a Hindu you are taught that you are paying for bad karma through repeated reincarnations until you get it right. As a Buddhist you are taught that you must go through 129 life-times to find enlightenment. Who the hell is right?! They all mean well I am sure, but the answer to who is right is found 'within' and not in religious institutions. It is not to be found in books or prophets. YOU have to look within!

In the journey of life, we all at some point ask the questions that everyone has about God. Is there a God? And if God does exist, whose religion is right? Well, there is an Infinite Intelligence that we call God. God is Spirit and God is Light. Therefore, God is Energy. God is a not an old, bearded man who sits in heaven somewhere looking and waiting for us to mess up so he can punish us. God is a loving being who is the life source energy of all things. God gives life to the universe (or cosmos) that is the result of his thoughts. These thoughts send off creative, vibrational energies that create the universe and all we see and cannot see. In other words, God created the beauty and wonder of the entire universe through just thinking and speaking it into creation with the power of thought! God is a loving energy that can reveal himself in a myriad of ways! God has and continues to communicate to us through all the energies of the universe. Everything God created has his energy and has the capacity to speak to us in many ways.

When God created the universe he created contrast. There is light and there is darkness. There is male and there is female. There is day and there is night. God created animals and humans. He created an amazing portfolio of different colors that can be seen in all of his creation. We live in a wonderful world of contrast! No two beings are alike and no two sunsets or sunrises are alike. We all have different personalities, physical traits, talents, gifts, and abilities. So what does this mean? Why did God allow this or create diversity and contrast?

God allowed contrast to create an environment whereby we can expand and develop. I call this the **Law of Opposites.** When we experience contrast of any type, good or bad, we move forward in our development. How else can we know what is good if we don't experience or see what we don't like? Contrast helps clarify what we like or dislike on many levels. It promotes growth through experiencing resistance and tension. Tension can propel us forward if we allow it to. It is just like the bodybuilder who builds his body through applying tension to the muscles to promote growth. Without the tension of life we would grow flaccid and weak. Life teaches us that trials, tribulations and afflictions try us, purify us and makes us strong! But if we resist this contrast we have a tendency to judge and condemn others for our own troubles. We turn bitter, feel hurt, get depressed, and experience fear and hopelessness.

We then get stuck in the muck and mire of contrast. But once we embrace the contrast we can move forward. How? By using the contrast to identify what we want and don't want. For example, when you get sick and tired of being sick and tired you can summon up the energy to move forward. **You have the choice! You have the power to change your life and move forward!**

Many Christians and religious **people are waiting for some magical moment** when they will be transformed in the twinkling of an eye. This is far from the truth. We were sent here to experience contrast and work out our salvation through tapping into the Light and Energy of God. This is more than just accepting Jesus Christ as your Savior. The Light and Energy that enabled Jesus can come to you and enable you to tap into the Life Source we call God! It is being baptized into the light and energy of God. Flowing with God is not saying a ritualistic prayer or going through some church ritual. It is the process where we attune to God, tap into God and get turned on by God. We will discuss how this happens in more detail later in this writing.

Christianity and other religions today, for the most part, are contorted systems of control, manipulation, domination, judgment, condemnation, rules and regulations set up by religious persons. Many of these religions are sincere, but they are sincerely mistaken. True religion points you to God and encourages you to tap into Life Source Energy or, if you like, the Spirit of Christ. Religion today has reduced God to a book, a church system, and a set of religious codes, rules and regulations that try to pound round circles (people) into square holes. Everyone is looked upon as lost sheep that need shepherds. They even have doctrinal police that run around and intimidate all who stray outside the play books. This leads to corruption, frustration, division, strife and fear. Some stay and conform, while others flee for their lives. Yes, there are good, well-meaning people in religious systems who try to do good and be good. I was a sincere Pastor at one time in these very religious systems. I was a sincere and had a great desire to know God and do his will. Most religious people desire the same. However, sincerity is often mistaken. Jesus came to cleanse the world of religion with the power of love! **God is Love!** After thousands of years of religious controversy, Jesus came to proclaim the good news that the God of this universe is a God of love.

Jesus wanted the world to know that the energy of God is Love. All that Jesus did was to help us see the true character of God in a sea of contrast! In the midst of all the religious conflict, political conflict, family conflict, spiritual conflict, mental conflict and physical conflict, Jesus came to give us new life by sharing the power of God with us all. Jesus overcame all the diseases of the world and promised that we could do likewise. In fact, Jesus said we would even do greater works than him!

By living in this world, we are all bouncing around in a sea of contrast. It is here we can find life by allowing the contrast to expand our spirits, minds and bodies to mature, grow and experience true bliss and happiness that comes from bouncing off the unhappy things we encounter in this world. What makes you happy is a clue to understanding what is right or wrong. We are not talking about doing bad things that hurt or harm others; we are talking about true joy and happiness that comes from experiencing good things. God is love and true happiness and joy are in harmony with the beauty and truths of God.

So how do we overcome and experience the bliss of God or the Life-Source of the Universe? I believe everyone, deep down, wants to experience the reality of God. But he is not found in a religion, a church, or a religious system. Most religion and religious systems do not point people to God; they call people to 'their' way of thinking. Religions say: Come to my tent, embrace my faith, accept my dogmas, obey my system, buy my products, and pay my bills. In return, they promise heaven and in some religious circles they promise some kind of reward. To reject 'their' faith always results in some form of punishment that leads you to be cast into Hell.

'True' religion always points you to God. It never points you to a system of rules and regulations. The essence and energy of God is found within! **The first step to knowing God** and experiencing Life Source Energy is to seek him inwardly. So many people look for God in all the wrong ways and places. I know I have. In fact, I wore myself to a frazzle trying to find God in churches, ministries, books, and everywhere but within. I finally came to the end of my rope. I still wanted to know God and learn more about the truth, but churches and religious systems were not leading me to him. This is when I started crying out to God. I showed God my frustration and let him know just how I felt about all that I had encountered. I told God that if I was to believe anything, he would have to show me directly. Otherwise, I wanted off the religious merry-go-round.

After this prayer, God showed up and began downloading all kinds of wonderful things to me that deep down inside, I always knew. **IT was there all the time!** I had been looking for love in all the wrong places! What did I learn? Well first, this handbook is all about my transformation. Everything I have written is what I have learned from God so far, and it is my desire that IT will help you get inspired enough to cry out to God also! I promise that if you seek you will find! So the **first thing** you need to do is seek God by looking inward and by getting real with him. Tell God how you feel. Then, ask him to open up the universe to you and expect God to answer your prayers. He will! Stop looking outward and look inward!

Second, spend time in prayer and meditation. Prayer is simply talking with God. There are many tools out there in the form of books, CD's, and other downloads that can assist you in prayer. Ask God to lead you to tools that will help you. But for now, just get alone with God and pray any way you like. God is not interested in ritual or religious form; he will honor your simple conversations with him. Then, learn to meditate. Meditation is the process of relaxing the mind and body so that you can tap into the Life-Source Energy God that flows inwardly from the universe. Mediation is where the magic begins! This writing will not cover all the wonderful ways we can tune in, but decide now that you will start praying and meditating. An easy thing to do would be to just pray and talk with God just like you would anyone for 5-15 minutes a day. Then just sit or lay down with your spine as straight as possible, and just concentrate on breathing and nothing else. Calm the mind, relax your body, and just enjoy the peace for 15 minutes.

Third, you might want to seek the fellowship of like-minded people who, like you, are on a similar journey. There are a lot more people like us than you think. And when you tell God and the universe you want to find these people, they will show up!

Fourth, I encourage you to set aside all your belief systems and ask God to reprogram you with the knowledge of the universe. Don't allow yourself to feel guilty about changing your belief systems. When we change into a person of God's love, we can do no wrong! Love would never harm or hurt anyone on purpose. It would not violate another person in anyway. Just love God, love yourself and love others. Ask God to show you his heart and mind and he will! In light of this, don't be critical of yourself and others. Forgive yourself and forgive others. Allow people to be who they are and release any anger, bitterness, strife, hatred, division, discouragement, or negative emotion. When it shows up, just let it go. Use it to move you in the opposite direction. Negative emotions serve as warning systems that things are not right. When we recognize the negativity, we can decide to move away from it. So use the negative to thrust you forward!

Fifth, I encourage you to see God as a God of love! God is love! God is Love! God is Love! **GOD IS LOVE!** Love is patient, kind, longsuffering, good, and forgiving. Love bears all things and hopes all things. Love never fails. Love never gives up. God is not out to judge and condemn you to hell. There is no such thing as a 'devil's hell' where God wants to burn and torture people forever and forever! God wants to give you life more abundantly. God wants to love on you as any parent would. Trust in this fact. **Embrace the God of love!** God's love is life-force energy that carries his essence everywhere and in everyone. God's love is ready to nurture you and provide you with everything you need! Believe and receive! See chapter eight for a study about hell.

We are spiritual life source beings who are on an exciting journey. We come to Earth as part of the adventure of becoming more aware and expanding God and the universe in a multiplicity of ways. The expansion of God and the universe occurs every time we think new thoughts and become more imaginative. God designed us in his image so that we could think, imagine, dream, create and expand spiritually, mentally, emotionally and physically. As we expand and produce in all these areas we cause the universe to expand. We are all extensions of God that have the ability to expand, grow and multiply the abundance of ourselves and the universe. There is nothing that can stop that expansion but you individually. You have the ability and choice to expand! We all have the ability to tap into God and find within ourselves the resources of the universe.

This journey can be activated at anytime. All we have to do is say yes! Yes to God. Yes to expanding! All you need is the willingness to embrace the unknown and make yourself available and responsive to God. Where you are is where you are, and that's ok. But where you are can be a bouncing off place to begin your journey of awareness. In the process of becoming aware we must let go of the past. Yes, we can learn from the past, but we cannot allow it to dictate who we are now. Our spiritual awakening is the process of understanding that we are spiritual beings of God's energy. As we become aware that we are part of a unified, multi-dimensional field of God's energy, we take the first step in our expansion.

Many people today are controlled, manipulated, and dominated by the thoughts and trends of society, religion, politics and other environmental influences. Most people go through life being a victim of these systems in one way or another. The transformation of our souls requires us to eliminate these influences and drop our own personal opinions. This can be painful and difficult. Change of this magnitude requires courage and willingness to go against the flow. The process of transformation is about becoming your true self. Your true self is Source Energy that wants to participate in the expansion of the universe. Your true self anticipates, with joyful expectation, to grow, mature, expand and be a part of the evolutionary expansion of the universe! **If you want to change the world, change yourself!**

In the transformation of our souls, we need to stop allowing ourselves to be controlled, manipulated, and dominated by the thoughts and systems of mankind. We have to stop identifying with society, cultural trends, political systems, religious systems, and even friends, family and racial identities. The collective beliefs of these systems have strong emotional attachments to our lives that may be holding us back. Is there a system you need to let go of? Are there people you need to let go of? What is holding you back? I am not saying that all these things are necessarily evil, but they most certainly are not profitable to the expansion and transformation process. No one person, system, or thing should have dominion over you. If you ever feel like you are being manipulated, controlled, dominated or demeaned, you will know that you need to break the spell it has on you or wants to put on you.

Also, if you are living in any kind of guilt or are holding on to any kind of bitterness, strife, hatred, division, unforgiveness or the like, you need to let it go now. All the failures of life are all done in ignorance. No one in their right mind desires to live in pain and misery or to inflict pain and misery. Once we are enlightened, we realize that failure is actually the place where we discover what works for us and what does not work. If things are not working out and your life seems to be a failure, then you are in a wonderful place.

Now, you can change your life by changing your mind. Your past thinking got you here and now your present thoughts can move you forward. Let it all go. Release yourself and release others. Forgive yourself and forgive others, for you all did not realize what you were doing. Just as Jesus hung on his cross and forgave his enemies, so must you. Jesus became an instrument of love that forgave all failure. God loves you and he is not holding your failures over your head or anyone else's. Embrace this love and freely offer it to all. God is love. The love of God is pure energy that embraces us all. So embrace God's love and become an agent of love. Now this does not mean that we are naive. Sometimes love requires us to move away from people and things that are not ready for this revelation. So relax and let go of things you have no control over. We can only be responsible for ourselves in life's journey.

Hopefully now, you are ready to take control of your life. You have discovered that the power is within you to transform and free yourself from the past. Your destiny is now in your hands! You realize now that no person, system or circumstance has power over you unless you give it control. You have decided to take full responsibility for your life and are empowered with the feeling of awareness that brings new life and energy to you. You now have the power to recognize negative thoughts and circumstances and filter them appropriately. You no longer allow yourself to become a victim of people, systems or circumstances. You now learn that you are more than all these things. So when things happen, you now use them to clarify life and bounce off of them more readily into a more positive direction.

As we learn that we can control our lives and circumstances we begin to become aware that God and the universe want to help and assist us with our thoughts and desires. We learn that the power of thought creates mental energy that is transmuted into reality - good or bad! I do not believe that anyone intentionally tries to create bad things with their thoughts. However, we must understand that negative attitudes, reactions, feelings and thoughts transmute into things that reflect and produce bad situations in our lives. Once we understand that, we can change! When we stop thinking negatively and stop living in the past or the future, we can live today! We can release all the negative energy in our lives. Once we stop living in fear and stop perpetuating lies in our lives we can break the spell of darkness and the clouds will give way to fresh air and sunlight. We learn from our mistakes and our failures. The trials and tribulations of life cleanse us from the error of wrong thinking and propel us into better places.

At this point, you learn how prayer, meditation, and visualization are so essential and meaningful. You are letting go and letting God! You are learning that even in chaos and darkness there is purpose. You are more relaxed and no longer fighting for your beliefs or arguing with people about theirs. You are less critical and judgmental of yourself and others. You recognize that we are all on a journey and we are all in different places, and that is ok! You no longer have materialistic addictions or unhealthy attachments to people or things. You no longer desire to have power over anyone or anything. You no longer have an ego that demands respect or attention. You are freer to live your life! In fact, you are more open and available to God to transform you. You are surrendering to the order of God's universe and ready to grow and expand.

As you surrender your ego to God, you make yourself available to become a vehicle and instrument of God. As you let go and let God, you become a channel for the energy of God to flow through. You have discovered your true self and the wonderful person you are in a healthy, non-egotistical way. Now you begin to flow in unity with God and realize your oneness with the universe. At this stage, life is good and things are going well. In fact, you feel more alive and you sense that you are in a place where life is not just happening, but you are happening! In this stage you pass through the good and bad circumstances of life with new insights and strength. Your prayer life has shifted from wanting things to wanting more of God. You seek to be used by God rather than using God. You now see with spiritual eyes and hear with spiritual ears. In the Bible, this is called "Christ in you!" It is the anointing, energy, and power of God flowing through you just as it did in Jesus. You're not a religious person, so to speak, you are an anointed one.

As an anointed one, you can now allow your true self to emerge. It is here you can easily do what you need to do and give up whatever needs to be shed to become more anointed and appointed by God. You are overcoming the ego and all the negative forces of life. You are releasing, as you are growing. Your life is lining up with God and you are becoming a unique expression of God in all power and glory. You are becoming an anointed god who can reflect the love and beauty of the universe. You are now expanding and causing God to expand! It is a place of love, beauty, goodness, peace, joy, and true bliss!

You need to question what you believe to be true about God. Most of what you believe is what you have been told by religious or non-religious people to believe or not to believe. I am not against God or well-meaning people. I am against religion! When Jesus walked the earth he was always battling religious people. In fact, it was religious people who had him crucified! Then, after he left this world, religious people hijacked his message and added religion to it! Jesus came to reveal the true character of God and the truth that sets us free! Jesus declared and demonstrated to the world that **GOD is LOVE!** Jesus taught that God is love and that if we loved as he loved, we would experience God and know God. It is that simple and all religious and non-religious people miss knowing God due to their misguided emotions, intellect and fears. I believe we are entering a new era of truth where God is being discovered once again outside all the religious and non-religious prejudices of the world.

Science and religion are a culmination of the quintessential search for truth. Religion and science have at times been antipodal. In this antithesis, truth has always been apparent in both as humanity has searched for answers to the mysteries of life. Deep within humanity is a desire to know absolute truth and both science and religion have tried to be the answer. Every person at some point has been in search for truth and answers to correct living and thinking. This very fact proves that truth does exist for all! Truth is available to us all and God and the universe are willing to reveal truth to all who sincerely desire to know it. That is why we need a **Science of Religion** that provides the exact knowledge and power to provide us with a life of love, peace, joy, satisfaction, and abundant living. We see abundance in the entire universe that provides for all creation the energy, power and truth to sustain it and bless it with all it needs to survive and thrive. Religious science is the culmination of the arts and sciences that unite the spiritual, physical, mental, and philosophical truths that are inherent in all things.

Religious science contains the best thoughts of the ages and presents these thoughts in a manner that bears witness with the truth. We are living in an exciting age of truth whereby we are seeing the dogmatism and superstitions of secular science and religion being eclipsed with the truth that sets us free. **Everyone has some kind of religion** whether it is scientific, philosophical or religious. Religion usually involves the belief in a god or system that attempts to answer the mysteries of life. Therefore everyone believes in something even if it is nothing! However, many times, these beliefs turn into dogmatism or superstition. The Universe desires for us to experience truth in such a way that it gives birth to living a life of abundance. We must avoid the pitfalls of dogmatism and superstition by keeping faith and reason in perfect balance and harmony.

We all wish to be right and know truth. Religion and science reflect the desire to have perfect knowledge and absolute truth. We live in a scientific and religious age that has a strong desire to know truth. That is why we need a Science of Religion that provides the best vehicle to discover and understand truth.

What is Religious Science? Religious science is the culmination and perfect blending of truth found in the practical science of understanding the physical, material, mental, metaphysical, psychological, philosophical, and ideological truths of life. The Divine Mind of God is the First Cause of all these concepts. They were born in the thought of God's mind. The human mind is an instrument through which the Divine Mind can transmute these thoughts. This Universal Spirit of Thought is inherent in all things and is the most subtle but most powerful energy of the universe. Religious Science is the way to attain the truth and understand the greatest ideals ever perceived. It provides a way for us to understand truth presented to us through the Divine Thoughts of God. Otherwise, we are left to our devices and thoughts that are isolated and not connected to the Divine Thoughts of the universe. If we are not connected to this Divine Energy, we will at best struggle in the duality of the divine and human. An unconnected mind creates struggle and conflict and for the most part, creates all the conflict and strife we see today in the world.

The relationship between God and humanity hinges on Universal Law and Spirituality. There is but One Mind in the Universe and all Truth is discovered by connecting to the Mind of God. Scientific and religious leaders have, for the most part, sincerely tried to discover the truth and teach the truth as they see it. It is an attempt to set down their own thoughts about God, life, science, religion, and the relationship between the visible and invisible. Humanity has throughout the age been attempting to work out a philosophy of life which deals with all the mysteries of life. That is why we need to be cautious about their teachings and revelations from a human stand point. All sacred writings and scientific discoveries should be studied with a spirit of wisdom and revelation. Knowledge of the Truth supersedes all natural understanding and interpretation. That is why there is always an element of Faith required. Faith is the belief that God will without doubt reveal the Truth. Faith is positive expectation! This belief requires faith apart from the ideologies of human reason. The receiving of Truth is a mental act that requires us to be receptive to the answer. Pre-conceived ideas have to be put aside as we tune into the Divine Mind of God who will guide us into all truth. The truth is within you and it is you! When we ask we will receive, when we seek we will find. Determine now to dislodge doubt, fear, unbelief, and willful ignorance. Determine now to trust in God and yourself. Let the journey of truth begin! I would like to encourage you to seek out the Life-Source God of the universe who is ready to embrace you with all his love and goodness. This Energy can renew and empower you and give you a wonderful life of beauty, love, goodness and purpose. It is yours for the asking! Ask and it shall be given, seek and you will find. Knock and the door to bliss will be opened. I pray that the God of peace and love will baptize you in his Energy to ignite the fires of love, joy, peace, goodness and beauty to fill you and bless you in every way!

Spiritual empowerment is the personal awakening that we are spiritual beings put here to evolve and expand. We all have the opportunity to awaken to the reality that we are spiritual beings in a biological body. The body likes to be in control and the spirit has to be awakened to its power. This is the process of becoming aware that we are more than humans with bodies. Once we become aware, we start a process of transformation that requires us to set our sights to the intention of heightened awareness. We should with joyful participation anticipate expansion, growth, maturity, evolution, and ecstasy!

Transformation is not for the weak, fearful, or cowards of real change. Transformation requires us to drop the opinions and mindsets that no longer serve the evolution of our souls. We all have been conditioned by our environmental 'race' factors such as family, friends, ethnicity, creed, education, politics, economics, philosophy, and religion. All of which can be powerful strongholds of belief that can keep us unaware and shackled to earthly ties. You do not have to be a spectator of life. The majority of people react to life and allow people and circumstances to shape them in every way. You do not have to be controlled by the tyranny of environmental influences. The good news is that you have the power to break these soul ties and choose to evolve and expand!

As spiritual beings we are unlimited in our journey to expand. There is no ceiling, no hindrance, and no obstacle that can hold you back but your own choice. This is true freedom! **The first step** is to make a choice to open up to learning more about **YOU**. There is so much more to know and understand. We live in a united, multi-dimensional field of awareness. Challenge yourself! Be open and observant, but don't be gullible. Expand your horizons. Embrace the universal spiritual domain of your existence. Expand your reality by expanding your perceptions.

There are three levels of perception. The first is the field of energy we call physical existence. This is called **Material Reality**. This is where we see, hear, smell, touch and experience life from the biological standpoint. Material Reality appears to be bound by time and space, cause and effect, and change. It is where most people seem to live and experience life on a biological level that is controlled by bodily functions and human relationships. The second field is called the **Virtual Domain**. This is the energy field of the mind that allows us to think, reason, imagine, dream, and process information. The energy of the mind and nervous system is invisible to the naked eye, but it is still real and powerful. The third field is the **Quantum Domain**. This is the energy field of the spirit where there is no time or limitation. Wholeness exists at every point. It is unbounded and is beyond birth and death. It is infinity.

On the **Quantum Level of Material Reality**, the atomic level of life is 99.99% space or what some call the Ether of the universe. In essence the whole universe is a vibrational energy field that creates a quantum mirage that our biological systems can experience. This field of energy is intelligent and interconnected within and without. We are a field of energy more than we are biological! We are 99.99% spiritual energy! The essence of our spirit comes from the breath of God or the vibratory energy of God that touches molecular structure and gives it life.

Life is an expression of God's organized, infinite intelligence. It is the playing out of God's dreams and visions that reflect His imagination and creativity. God creates through intellect, reason, design, imagination, dreams, desire and creativity that brings love and joy into existence. We are spiritual beings also created in God's image to reflect God in the same way! Our spirit energy is experiencing life in a magnificent biological body that is truly an amazing machine of atoms, molecules, cells, systems and all else we are made up of. It is a technological wonder! That is how and why the body is interconnected in the spiritual, physical, and mental fields of life. As God is a field of energy and a reflection of material reality that operates in the Virtual domain, **so are we**. We are a threefold work of life! We are a spiritual being designed by God to live in a physical body that makes us a living soul on earth.

Once we begin to understand these principles, **we open ourselves up** to expansion, growth, and change! It is here we can escape the prison of conditioning that we learned from well-meaning parents, friends, educators, religious leaders, politicians, philosophical systems, and all else that has shaped our minds. We can now replace these old ways with new life affirming ways. Whenever we choose to make a change in any way, we ultimately effect more change to come. Embrace your spiritual domain and you will expand your horizons. Embracing your spiritual essence allows you to come into union with your true self. Knowing one's self is the pathway to experience the reality of life. This pursuit allows us to integrate our body to cooperate with our spirit so that we can create spontaneous harmony within and without! Your desires begin here to unite and you begin to blossom with godly intuition, insight, imagination, creativity, wisdom, knowledge, intimacy and harmony. This harmony energizes us and brings meaning and purpose to life!

This is the first step in being empowered. You make a choice to change. This is where you begin to wake up and reset your reference points from the experiences that have formed you up to this point. Until now you have been an observer, a spectator, and an eyewitness to life based on your environmental experiences. Reality is always the result of perception which involves the act of attention and interpretation. That is why our reference points have to be reset and reprogrammed. The process of awakening and being resurrected from the rudiments of the world requires the transformation of our material reality through spiritual awakening. In spiritual language this is referred to as regeneration. It is changing and resetting the way you think and act. **It is the process of knowing who you are!**

Tuning in to your true self destroys the competition of duality. Most people desire absolute truth with which they can direct their lives. This sets the stage in the material world for competition, divisiveness, strife, arguments, hatred, conflict, and all contradictory systems of belief. When we become Cosmic-conscious we no longer see duality but harmony. You begin to realize that who you are in spirit is more important than what you think you are. Self-realization is not about keeping a set of rules and regulations some person or system has come up with to please some god. Enlightenment is content with being and living in the present moment with no stress or conflict. If you are living in conflict, you are not in tune with your true self. When we embrace the energy, the light, and the love of our true self, we awaken to truth that sets us free! Free from all negativity and conflict.

Step Two in Spiritual Empowerment is the choice to stop being a drifter who depends on others to think for you. A drifter is someone who has allowed life to control them and guide them. The drifter lacks the confidence to think for himself, to set goals for himself, to dream for himself, or act on his own ability to live life in all confidence. Drifters tend to be broke, in debt, sick, depressed, in pain, moody, lacking self-control and discipline, narrow-minded, intolerant, superficial, judgmental, overweight and out of shape, critical, jealous and envious, takers not givers, and many times addicted to something good or bad.

Empowered people who are enlightened are self-confident people who are goal directed and on a divine mission to serve and be productive. Empowered people think life is a wonderful place to grow and expand. Failure is seen as an opportunity to grow and change. They choose to be in control of their lives and refuse to be manipulated, dominated or controlled by anyone or anything. They tend to be magnetic, compassionate, passionate, loving, caring, and cheer for others to succeed and be themselves.

The pathway to empowerment is taking personal responsibility for your own enlightenment! Drifters are usually victim conscious and believe that they are controlled by outside forces. Drifters like to make excuses and blame others for their failures. Stop playing the victim game and stop listening to people who perpetuate negative energy and thoughts. Don't be easily manipulated and influenced by people, books, or systems of belief. Stop being race conscious. Stop being influenced by the collective beliefs of any group of people. Drifters live from one reaction to another trying to cope and defend their previously digested thoughts from relationships, belief systems, and perceptions on the material level. Are you trying to maintain the status quo? Are you always reacting? Do you have something to defend?

When we become aware that we have followed the road of a drifter we can now take responsibility to think for our self and control our own thoughts. We all at one time suffered from ignorance! So forgive yourself for being a victim and forgive those who have victimized you. Release any anger, bitterness or ill feelings in regard to this matter. After all, we would not be victims or victimizers if we really knew better! This means we have to stop telling the same old victim stories over and over! Release the negativity and stop talking about your ignorance and the ignorance of others! Forgive, forget and move on! Identify any of these things and let go of them. Let go and let your true self expand! The old powers are vanquished, released and no longer have the power to influence you. Release yourself and release others from animosity, resentment, blame, hate, revenge, and division. In the future, whenever you feel like a drifter, observe the feelings and acknowledge that this is the old materialistic person thinking and not you're true empowered self. Then you can shift your thinking to transformation, expansion, and moving forward. It's ok to feel negative but recognize the negative, adjust, and move away from it.

Step three in Spiritual Empowerment is releasing fear. Fear is a negative energy that controls and manipulates a material conscious person. Much of the world's problems center around things that people fear and people who use these fears to control people! People desire the basic needs of life and fear losing them. People fear many things and whatever you fear grows stronger if you think about it. What you resist will persist! Fear attracts fear. The feeling of fear is a negative energy that weakens you and will defeat you if you don't cast it away.

Trust in your true self empowers you to know that fear is a negative energy that goes against the positive energy of the universe. Fear energy encourages negative actions and reactions. It can cause us to steal, kill, destroy, control, manipulate, and fall deeper into negativity. When we are living in the frustration and the energy of fear we begin to fear things like ill health, poverty, loss of freedom, loss of love, and all else that we hold precious. This is how dictators, governments, politicians, religious leaders, parents, educators, etc. gain control over people. When we energize fear, we make our self susceptible to the thoughts and control of others.

Trusting in love casts off all fear! When we are attuned to our true self we know we are not material beings in need of material things. We are spiritual beings that need only our connection to our spirit essence and the energy of the universe. When we are aware and empowered, we don't need someone else to think for us or take control of us. **The power of thought is a mental energy** that can change your spiritual circumstances. You are where you are because of your thoughts! Thoughts are mental energy that ultimately becomes our reality. Thoughts transmute your beliefs, your speech, and your behavior and combine to create your present life. No, no one consciously or purposely invites fear, death, illness, poverty, loss, etc into their life. However, ignorance and material connections on unconscious levels can invite and set up conditions for things like this to manifest. As long as we walk in fear, doubt, worry, and negativity we attract the same.

The key is to not to start blaming and play the victim. Just chalk it up as ignorance and walk in the new awareness. Allow the fear to propel you forward. Once you know what does not work and what you don't like, you can move away from it. As we take dominion over fear we can release the negative energy that is obstructing the inner beauty and splendor of our spiritual essence! Whenever we feel guilty or cast blame, we are not attuned to our spiritual self. Through prayer, meditation, affirmations and positive thinking you enlighten yourself and empower yourself to overcome. The lessons of life help us evolve, grow, and expand. Relax when things happen and don't get caught up in self critical judgments that beat you down. Learn that even in chaos and darkness there is purpose behind it. All things work for our good! Infinite Intelligence and the universe are always on our side! God is love and nothing can separate us from that love that energizes the entire universe or cosmos! **God is Energy!**

Step four in Spiritual Empowerment is learning to live in the spiritual energy of the cosmos spontaneously. As you attune with your true self you come into harmony with the cosmos, and you become an extension of the cosmos. You discover your true self and surrender your life and ego to Infinite Intelligence. You are a vehicle for Infinite Intelligence, an instrument to be tuned and played, a channel for the cosmos to work through. Things begin to happen through you as you become available to the cosmos. Life flows effortlessly and with all bountifulness. You enact the talents, gifts and abilities given to you. You are no longer concerned about self or attached to the material. You live in all three dimensions of life in all harmony and peace. Yes, there may be times of darkness but you just embrace it and walk through it. Right before a breakthrough there can be a breakdown, a releasing of negative energy, to make way for new positive energy that inspires you to new heights, insights and strength. You no longer wonder what to do; you are seeking to be used by the cosmos as you attune to your true self. Your intuitive faculties are more sensitive and aware. You see with spiritual eyes, you hear with spiritual ears, and all your senses are attuned to the higher power within.

The Secret to life is in you! This is a mystical truth that empowers us and enlightens us to the truth of who we are and where we are going. It is a spirit of wisdom and revelation in the knowledge of our self in relationship to the universe. So many people are looking for answers in a church building, a religious temple or synagogue. Many believe they will only know or experience truth in death or some future event. In the bible, Jesus the Anointed One came to show us the way, the truth and the light. Jesus was empowered by Infinite Intelligence to be the example we could all follow and know the way. Calling on Jesus is calling on a pattern, not a person. Jesus said follow me, not cling to me and ride on my shoulders into heaven. Jesus always pointed us and guided us to look within. Jesus was one with himself and the cosmos and desired for us to be also. Yes, he died in the hands of an angry mob of religious and political people. Jesus death and his resurrection prove that we all can be attuned to our spiritual reality also. Jesus always desired for us to be one with Infinite Intelligence. So yes, it is good to believe in Jesus the Anointed, but it is important to know that saying a prayer in Jesus name is not enough. The life and ministry of Christ was to provide an example on many levels for us to call upon! However, enlightenment and empowerment will only happen when we attune to within and walk the pathway of an anointed. The power in life is found within. As Jesus overcame the material world of reality, so can we! We just have to stop looking outward and start looking inward.

So how do we attune? How do we become empowered? Prayer and meditation is one tool for us to use to attune. We must look inward during this time. We have to stop using our intellect or emotions and discover the true self that is found within. This may require us to practice prayer and meditation on a daily, monthly, and yearly basis. Our true self is always there to lead and guide us into all truth; it is a still small voice that transcends the intellect and emotion of our biological bodies. Fellowship with enlightened ones and those desiring to be empowered is also a way to stay attuned. Who you hang out with and who you fellowship with always will affect who you are. It is also important to study and educate yourself with the teachings of enlightened and empowered ones. What you read and watch effects who you are. And last but not least, a steady diet and a regiment of daily affirmations that confirm who you are and what you are affect your spiritual empowerment. What you say affects who you are! When we begin to attune we begin to live spiritually sensitive lives that stay connected with the higher self and the higher dimensions of God and the universe. You attune inwardly to the qualities of Infinite Intelligence and begin to manifest love, peace, joy, goodness, and beauty! You will be at peace and content. You will realize all you need to know. **YOU will be empowered! You will know YOU!**

Spiritual Affirmations

I am pure spirit that was, is, and always will be. In the present moment, I am an eternal being in a biological body that I now use to grow and expand. I am made in the image of God and I reflect and co-create as a god on earth. I enjoy and love my life! As pure spirit, I am eternal.

I am one with God and the Universe. God and the Universe are always conspiring to empower me to be successful in all of my life's dreams, visions and goals. In this I am confident and have the faith to believe that all things are working for my good.

I am inspired to aspire so that as I aspire, I inspire! Each day is a resurrection day of life that overcomes all darkness and brings forth resurrection power in all I do and say. God's power indwells me and God's mind, the Christ-Conscience of the Universe, guides me into all truth.

God is Love and I am loved. God loves me unconditionally and is always ready, willing, and able to empower me with all that I need. I love God and God loves me. I love people as God loves people. Love is always patient, kind, long-suffering, forgiving, merciful, and never fails. God will never fail me and I am destined to overcome all failure.

The Infinite creative power of God lies within me. The kingdom and power of God is within me and I give thanks to God who gives me the power to create, achieve, and prosper in every way. There is no lack with God and no limitation within the Divine Laws of Establishment. Therefore, I lack nothing and am not limited within this law. I am in harmony with the laws of God.

I control my thinking. I attract into my life all good through positive thoughts and affirmations. I repel all negative thoughts and reject all ideas of lack, disease, pain, sorrow, fear, worry, and all ill feelings. I am positive and affirm that the power of God enables me to aspire!

I choose LIFE! I view life through the lens of **LOVE**! I respond to life with love instead of reacting to life.

I am enlightened! My personal commitment is to support all initiatives that ignite a dynamic process for enlightenment on a personal and global basis.

I believe in the power of LOVE! Love is divine, living energy of unparalleled might and magnificence. Love is my true state of being. This belief manifests itself in all love, joy, peace and harmony. Love molds and holds the universe together!

I believe in the power of Choice! Life is a matter of choice. My life is a direct result of my choices. From my choices the quality of my life manifests. What I sow, I reap.

I believe in the power of Belief! Faith is the substance of things we anticipate and the evidence of things not manifested. I have faith in God and I have faith to believe all things are possible in God. According to my faith, so it is. I am confident in God and confident in myself to think confident thoughts that empower me. I have the faith that I can move mountains.

I believe in the power of Prayer! Prayer gives me the ability to draw from the spiritual realms the strength and inspiration my mind needs to behold the powers of God. My prayers positively direct my life through positive intentions, affirmations, and purpose driven thoughts and actions. What I visualize in prayer will be actualized!

I am a great, powerful and mighty spiritual being of light that originates from the Life-Source Energy of God. I am flawless. I am the beautiful reflection of my Divine Parentage. No matter what my humanness portrays, my identity as spiritual perfection is intact. I am the essence of the Great I Am. I am the magnificent expression of universal perfection!

I am free to choose happiness, enlightenment, and higher thought, no matter what circumstances challenge me. I protect and encourage my right to choose the best in myself, for myself, and for others, always!

It is my destiny to serve as a vessel for the Light of Love! I am on a holy mission toward the attainment of truth and spiritual enlightenment. I seek to aspire so that I may inspire!

I am blessed with abundant gifts. The Spirit of God had enabled and empowered me with abundant gifts and talents. It is part of my earth assignment to recognize, strengthen, and utilize these gifts to my highest potential, for the good of all. Therefore, I devote my divine gifts and talents to the upliftment of humankind. Every soul is born into this world with a talent and a task, a memory and a mission; and everyone arrives with a gift and a goal.

I am present NOW! I seize the moment and the power and glory of the Spirit that is evidenced in my exuberance for life. I bask in the sparkle of the passionate nature of God and the Universe. In all ways, I seek to bring exuberance to my life's tasks, my personal being, and my sacred space.

I know where I want to go and what I want to achieve. My dreams are God's dreams and there are no challenges that can stop me. Life is not a race but a journey to be savored each step of the way!

No life is ever wasted. Today, I take time to remember loved ones, and am grateful for their priceless gifts and what their lives have bequeathed me.

I am here to assist God in the expansion of Divine Consciousness. I inspire others to love, encourage them to dream, and empower them to keep hope alive. I look for opportunities to serve and help others! The more I love, the greater my capacity to do so.

Infinite Spirit, I acknowledge your Infinite Intelligence that permeates all of life. I acknowledge Your Presence, Your Life, Your Light, and Your Glory.

I affirm your essence and draw upon thy Light and Energy to fill me with all love, joy, peace, goodness, health, vitality, energy, and power to live life to its fullest extent! Your Light moves through me to cleanse me, nourish me, heal me, restore me, purify me, encourage me, and sustain me in every area of my life: spirit, mind, body, emotions, and in every way.

I am open and receptive to all the Good and Abundance of the Universe. I am open and receptive to new things, new ideas, new avenues of income, new and unexpected sources of life. I am an unlimited being accepting from an unlimited God in an unlimited way! I give thanks for the unlimited increase in my mind, my body, my spirit, my life, my affairs, my money and all else that is increasing, expanding and being blessed in all ways. Your thoughts come to me clearly and with clarity. I am blessed beyond measure in every way. I am strong, healthy, magnetic and living an **ageless life of beauty.**

You supply all my needs. I am prospering in every way. Every day, in every way, I am getting better in every way! Money comes to me quickly, under grace in perfect ways, to supply my every need, my every dream, my every vision, my every undertaking!!! As my Loving Parent, You desire to give me the desires of my heart, supply my every need, and care for me in every way. Every plan not planned by you, will be dissolved and dissipated quickly, so that, I can move forward. Divine plans are orchestrated by you and sent to me in the Light of Your Glory.

Divine Love now dissolves and dissipates every wrong condition in my life. I release grief, pain, anger, resentment, and all negativity from my life.

I forgive myself because **God loves me** and God has forgiven me. I release myself from all my failures and negativity. I am loosed of all the cords of mistakes that have bound me up. My failures have been erased. My knots are untangled. I am scrubbed free from all offences, hurts, shame, and embarrassments. I now release the cords of mistakes of others and freely forgive and release others from all wrong doings. I forgive the unforgivable and commit them into Thy hands. You keep me out of trouble, falsehood, deception, delusion, vacillation, deceit, injustice, harmful circumstances, and all that holds me back. Enable me to overcome and rise up into all victory! **Divine Love** now heals me, restores me, fills me, and encourages me and those I contact. Every cell in my body is filled with Your Light, Your Love, and Your Presence! In Thy presence all is perfect, all is well, and all is whole. I am one with you and our wills move together in Divine cooperation. I am an instrument that is tuned and orchestrated for your purposes. So be IT!

Chapter Two

Mental Life

The mind is a powerful mechanism that plays a major role in our success. God gave us a brain with the capacity to think, imagine, reason and solve. We possess intellect and wisdom. We have creativity and the ability to manufacture thoughts and ideas. Our minds are powerful computers that can be programmed and trained to perform great things! That is why if we plan on living a successful life we have to be transformed with the renewing of our minds. This comes through what we read and by what we listen to and see with our eyes. Our minds have to be programmed with correct thinking. As we discussed in the spiritual part of this book, this requires us to challenge our environmental influences and reset our thinking. Your mind has had a lot of garbage fed to it over the years and it needs to be re-programmed. Be selective in whom and what you allow to influence your life. There are well meaning people who think they have all the answers. They may have some but they may not have them all. Look at their life and see if what they are is what you want to be. If not, you may need to find someone who is succeeding in the area of life in which you are looking for help. Be a fruit inspector. Don't be foolish and allow anyone to influence your life that is not where you want to be. You can love everyone but you may not want to be like them in every way. Learn from everybody. It may be a lesson on what to do or what not to do!

The mind of a person is the most powerful computer on earth. God designed the mind to direct and sustain all biological and organic functions of the body through the subconscious mind. The source of all direction and coordination of body functions, thoughts, facts, and knowledge are stored there and operate automatically based on its God-given program and the programming of our subconscious mind. The subconscious mind is also telepathic and has the capacity to sense and pick up things in the spiritual and physical dimension of the cosmos. The brain can and does communicate with God, others and the cosmos.

The conscious mind has the power of directing thoughts, reasoning, emotion, will-power, imagination, decision-making, moral consciousness, knowledge and creativity. Through our intelligence our thought life can be directed through self-discipline. Self-discipline is attained through the control of thought habits. You are where you are and what you are because of the habits of thought. Your thoughts are what you think about due to the things you feed your brain. (Books, magazines, music, literature, the Bible, sacred writings, friends, family and associates) God gave us the power of choice and the unchallengeable right to control our minds, thoughts and habits. Every man is a bundle of habits. Self-discipline is the only means by which one's habits of thought can be controlled and directed. The potential of the human mind is beyond comprehension. Man has the capacity and ability through faith, will-power and God's Spirit to modify, change and control the nature of his thoughts, and in doing so, change one's life in a positive way!

Negative thoughts lead to self-destruction and positive thoughts lead to prosperity. We can open our minds to negativity or we can open our minds to the positive thoughts of God. The greatest need is recognizing our ability to live an abundant life of prosperity. Whatever stays on our min affects our emotions, memory, telepathic powers, moral conscience, imagination, reason, intelligence and will power in either a positive or negative way. That is why the mind has to be transformed and renewed.

Throughout our life we have been subjected to many things that have subconsciously programmed who we are. Through our five senses of sight, sound, taste, smell and touch we have been shaped into who we are and where we are in life. What we have listened to, read and seen has shaped us. What we have heard and said has impacted our actions and reactions. What we have felt, smelled and tasted has caused us to be prejudice. All of these memories (storage banks), factors and variables can make us closed-minded or receptive to both good and evil. Top this off with the sixth sense of the brain that is receiving and broadcasting positive or negative energy that can influence us either way. The mind is the greatest battlefield we will ever face. It is in this war zone that all the issues of life are won or lost. The power to overcome our mind, re-program it, transform it and be renewed can only come about through faith, discipline, determination, and yielding to the Spirit of God and the positive energy of the Universe.

There is a divine law that states 'what you sow is what you reap. The mind is a garden that has to be cultivated, watered, and weeded before there is a harvest. What we read, study, ponder, meditate upon, speak about, and trust in is sowing good seed or bad seed that will bring forth either a good crop or bad crop. This is why we must learn what to say and what not to say. By your words you are justified and by your words you are condemned. Death and life are in the power of the tongue. Whatever you sow with the tongue is what you reap. The power of the spoken word is a law more powerful than the law of gravity. What you say and speak affects who you are and who you are becoming! Do not be snared by the words of your mouth. Speak life and you will have life. The creative power of the tongue is real and has great consequences in our lives. You can speak your way into life or death. That is why 'affirmations' are a huge part of transforming your mind. You need to be speaking correctly and train your mind to listen to the new information so that it will reprogram the software and eliminate all the viruses of your mind.

The mind must be transformed, renewed and reprogrammed. A diseased mind will have a host of beasts that can cause depression, cynicism, negativity, irritability, ungratefulness, criticalness, resentment, worry, anxiety, double-mindedness, distress, guilt, excessive grief, hopelessness, despair, anger, hatred, discord, dishonesty, evil thoughts, confusion and all kinds of perversities. These beasts are like cancer cells that steal, destroy and kill you and those around you. The diseased mind withholds love, holds on to past hurts, criticisms, injuries and refuses to turn away from these awful beasts. The end result is a defeated, unhappy and negative person. These diseased attitudes are a result of a lifetime of negative emotions that have been programmed deep into the subconscious mind. You are the sum total of your past, present and future thoughts. Thoughts are powerful and affect every cell, nerve, gland, organ and system in your body. This is why the mind is the biggest battlefield in your life. Your mind has to be renewed day by day and is in a life-long process of transformation. The mind has to be trained and programmed every day. Whatever we put in our minds affects our thoughts. Your thoughts affect your feelings. Your feelings affect your actions. Your actions affect who you are and where you are in life. As we change what we program our mind with, we change our attitudes. As we change our attitudes, we change our feelings. As we change our feelings, we change our attitudes.

As we change our attitudes our lives change based on what has been programmed into our minds. When we change our choices in life we react differently to our environment. As we change our thoughts and habits we can take control of our lives. The choice is yours. Start today to reprogram your brain with things that are pure, just, true, honorable, right, gracious, excellent, praiseworthy, godly and constructive. Reject the negative things of life and seek a life of true success. Read books and listen to audio programs that feed your mind with good things. Associate with people who are going where you want to go. Think, dream and imagine that you are successful in every way! Believe in your God-given talents and abilities. You are made in His image to take dominion! Don't listen to losers or anyone who discourages you. Don't let anybody rob you of your God-given right to succeed. Take control of your life or somebody else will. Don't sell your birthright for a mess of pottage. You are a special person who deserves to live life to its fullest extent. IT is your destiny.

It's time to write out a mission statement and set some goals to improve your mind. What are you going to program your mind with? When will you take the time to re-program your mind? You may need to turn off the TV, iPod, or the radio. You may need to change your friends and associations and find new ones that are more positive and success conscious. You may need to invest in some books and audio materials. Are you furthering your skills and abilities to get ahead in your chosen profession? Do you need to change professions? Do you need to improve your talents, skills and abilities? How can you improve yourself? Work out a plan. Set some goals. Write out some decrees. Take action! Program your mind to succeed. God gave you a brain! Go use it to expand your talents and abilities.. Cast down the stinking thinking thoughts that are destroying your life and feed your mind with good things. You can reprogram your mind and change your life! Whatever you imagine, desire, believe in, and act enthusiastically upon will inevitably come to pass!

The Law of Thought is a law that states that 'as a man thinks, so he is'! This is why it is imperative for you have the confidence to believe that YOU have the ability to achieve the object of your definite purpose in life. It is therefore necessary that you require yourself to be persistent and take continuous action towards ITS attainment. This law promises that the dominating thoughts of your mind will eventually reproduce themselves in some type of outward action and physical reality. This is why you need a vision, a dream and a burning desire of what IT is you want to achieve. The art of manifesting your desires is discovered by simply following these steps:

Step One: Begin with the End in Mind. The first step in manifesting your desires is to know what your desire is! A desire must be so vivid and real that you have already experienced the emotion and sensation of that desire beforehand. A desire is only a wish if you do not know exactly what you desire and have it so engrained in your spirit, mind and body that there is no doubt or fear of not having that desire. The reason why so many people never accomplish their goals and desires is because they do not have a burning desire that they are consumed with. Successful people are those who have a definite desire that is burning in their bones like fire!

People, who have a wish and are only giving something a try, usually fail and give up. Winners fail forward and keep on keeping on no matter what! So begin with the end in mind and work your way backwards to the things that have to be done for your desires to become a physical reality. If you do not have any burning desires, then now is the time to take the time and find some! How do you find them? By getting alone and searching your heart, soul, and mind to reveal to you what you really desire! Ask yourself, if there were no obstacles of any kind to stop you, what you would like to do, have, or accomplish in life? Then get a piece of paper and start writing down all your thoughts, dreams, and desires. After you write them down, then examine them all and decide which ones you really desire the most. Keep narrowing down your desires until the only ones left are the ones that excite you, motivate you, and would truly make you happy and fulfilled! After you have decided what dreams and desires you can truly commit to, then it is time to write down those dreams and desires in vivid detail. Then pray, meditate and experience your desires in your imagination. Feel the emotions that you would expect to experience when your dreams come true! Smell, hear, taste, feel, see and embrace your desires! This is the first step. Begin with the end in your mind!

Step Two: Take Full Responsibility for Your Desires! The second step in manifesting your desires is to take full responsibility for your desires. Like it or not, your life is a reflection of your choices and not someone else's. Stop believing that life is doing something to you and that your circumstances are the result of fate. Stop playing the victim and stop feeling sorry for yourself. Victim conscious people are influenced by the dreams and desires of others rather than their own. Stop blaming people and circumstances and take personal responsibility for your life. Taking personal responsibility for our lives makes us aware that we control our thoughts, emotions and destiny. When we are aware, we are in control and can observe our life and change it if we desire to! Stop blaming people, circumstances and holding on to the past. Stop beating the drum of the past or it will continue to vibrate within and around you to produce your past perceptions and beliefs. Forgive and forget the past things that have victimized you. Forgive yourself, forgive others, and release all blame.

The past has no authority over you! Affirm that your destiny is in your own hands. Take the power of personal responsibility and manifest your desires!

Step Three: Take Control of Your Thoughts! The third step in manifesting your desires is to take control of your thoughts. Thoughts are mental energy that ultimately becomes our life experience. Thoughts transmute into your life spiritually, physically, mentally and ultimately create your life experiences. Life is not a life of chance and fate. Nothing happens by chance. Life is a direct result of your thoughts! The first resistance that comes up in this awareness is the feeling of why would anyone invite negative circumstances into their life? No one in their right mind would purposely invite tragedy, sickness, or hardship into their life! However, we all do, unconsciously and in ignorance, invite and set up conditions for things like this to show up. Whenever we are thinking and walking in fear, doubt, worry, guilt, judgment, condemnation, negativity, and the like, we draw and attract negativity. The Law of Manifestation teaches us that we can take dominion over our thoughts and that we have the ability and power to release and block all negativity. Negativity blocks our desires and more importantly our inner beauty and splendor of God and the universe. Overcoming negativity helps us to evolve, expand, grow, and mature. The fires of life purify and clarify. They serve as a bouncing off place to move away from victimization. Therefore control your thoughts, control your emotions and ordain your destiny!

Step Four: Prayerize as you Visualize and you will Actualize! The fourth step is to practice and develop an affirmative prayer life. Prayer is the process of affirming and stating in the present your visualized desires from step one. Never beg or wish. Have the faith to believe that what you have conceived of is already a done deal. You have planted, watered and tilled and the harvest is coming! Hope is more than wishing. Hope is positive expectation! Therefore we must pray in the "I AM" power of God. State your desires with the mantra: 'I am'. Prayer is accepting that God will grant the desires of your heart and that you need not beg or wish any more. It is done. So be it. Amen!

When you let go of being a victim and stop getting caught up in materialism, self-centeredness, greed, power, judging, criticizing, and all negativity, everything you do becomes about the evolution and expansion of your soul, God and the universe. When you surrender to the order of God's universe you become a participant of the universe by expressing God's energy and light. By letting go of your ego (edging God out!) you let God manifest through you. At this point, you become available to God and the Universe to evolve through you! You learn that even in chaos and darkness there is purpose behind everything. You stop being concerned about what others say, think, or do and start living out your own dreams and desires. Life begins to just happen as you become a vehicle through which life has its way with you. You discover and activate your own unique self. This activates the life source energy of God to be a beneficial presence on earth as it is in heaven! You can now flow in the cosmic energy of God and the Universe. This is why we need to pray, affirm and meditate. Praying and meditating empowers us from within to enter the vortex of God's energy and re-charge, regenerate, tune in, tap in and get turned on for God!

As you attune, you start becoming and transforming into an expression of God. Prayer and meditation begins to be a place you look forward to! Life will begin to revolve around this blissful time. Prayer and meditation allows life to just happen through you with new insights and strength. Yes, there will be times of struggle, but you learn to walk through it. In fact, right before a breakthrough there will be a breakdown and a release that leads to transformation. You are no longer telling or asking God to do things for you, but you are seeking to be used as God, the higher power found within you. It is Christ in you the hope of glory! It is God in you. **It is God being you!**

Take time to get into the Vortex of God by praying and meditating and offering yourself to God. Affirm that you have spiritual eyes to see and spiritual ears to hear. Ask yourself what desires need to emerge from within that you know harmonize and flow with God and the universe? Ask yourself if these desires and visions are in alignment with your talents, gifts and abilities given to you by God? Ask yourself if there is anything you need to release in order to manifest the desires? Ask yourself if you are willing to say yes to your God-given desires? If you are, then give thanks to God for giving you the desires of your heart, the ability and power to accomplish them, and the joy that comes from living them. Now, go back to step one and write the vision you desire to manifest and begin with the end in mind!

As I conclude this chapter I believe it is imperative that we understand the **Personality Dynamics** of ourselves and others. This world needs people who understand themselves and other people mentally. This will help us all reach our full potential. There are some basic principles of understanding yourself and other people that can enhance your life so that you can help yourself and others have less stress and enjoy life in a more productive way. The first principle is learning to understand yourself and being aware of your personality style. The second is learning to understand others. The third is learning to accept yourself and others. The fourth is learning how to adjust yourself and accommodate others. The fifth is learning that differences are good! The sixth is learning not to take things personally. The seventh is learning that there is no such thing as perfection in human beings. And finally, learn how to see life as an adventure with multiple opportunities to overcome obstacles and challenges.

The science of defining and understanding personality style can be traced back to Hypocrites, the father of modern medicine. Hypocrites concluded that there were four behavior styles defined by the terms choleric, sanguine, phlegmatic and melancholy. Since Hypocrites, the science of understanding personality dynamics and styles has evolved and been developed with more research. There are a number of scientific models used in determining and predicting human behavior based on personality profiles. The way a person thinks, feels and acts can be determined and predicted by these profiles. Distinctive patterns of behavior can be identified and classified as passive, assertive, outgoing, reserved or aggressive.

The scientific model used in this handbook is based on the human behavior model developed by Dr. William Marston. Dr. Marston devised the **'DISC'** model that identifies four distinctive patterns of behavior.

These four models revolve around outgoing or reserved behavior that can be task or people directed. It is in my opinion that the DISC model is the easiest to understand and remember of all the personality profiles available today. The DISC model is a tool that can revolutionize your life and the lives of people you come in contact with everyday.

The DISC model defines four basic personality styles that are sometimes called temperaments. The four basic styles are four personality traits that we can all have. We can be a blend of them all but there is usually one basic trait that dominates the other traits we possess. Therefore, when we discover our basic style we can learn how to improve our personality and balance strengths and weaknesses in a positive way. The DISC model splits the four basic personality styles into two basic patterns of behavior we would define as an extrovert and an introvert. Some people are more active and/or outgoing and some are more passive and reserved. This will help you understand why some people are introverted but like to be around people and why some are introverted and are not comfortable around people. Some people are active but not people oriented. Some people are outgoing but not motivated or driven to accomplish a task. Personality traits can vary in intensity and style. We are 'wired' differently and no two people are exactly alike. However, we will find similarities and patterns that are duplicated in people whose personality styles are characteristically the same. In general, we will either be **outgoing** or **reserved** in our personality style while being either **task oriented** or **people oriented**.

In the DISC model the acrostic letters **D, I, S, and C** define the four basic personality styles. One of these letters with blends and sub-traits of one or more of the other letters define a person's personality. These characteristics control who we are, how we act, what we do and where we are more comfortable in life. Once we identify our personality styles we can then learn what our strengths and weaknesses are. This in turn can help us improve who we are and cause us to make the necessary changes we need to implement to enhance our personalities. When we learn to understand ourselves, we can learn to be better people in all areas of our lives. When we understand ourselves in light of the DISC model, we can better understand others. When we understand others we recognize our differences in a positive light which can cause us to have less conflict and stress in our relationships. This model will enhance your ability to perform better in any of the six areas discussed in this handbook.

The first personality style we will define is the **D personality**. The D is a person who is a task-oriented and assertive individual who is driven and motivated to get things done. D's tend to be **dominating** people who are **determined** to accomplish their tasks. Their focus can cause them to ignore people and circumstances when they are setting out to do something. They are usually **decisive** and confront issues head on. They may seem forceful and even **dictatorial**. D personalities are original thinkers who are usually visionaries who like to lead and charge ahead. D's are independent and sometimes **defiant**. They may push the limits and boundaries in their drive to get the job done. D's are gutsy, chance-takers that will forcefully take charge and push forward. D's are natural born leaders who can make decisions and take charge of situations.

The strengths of D personalities can become their weaknesses if they push their personality to the extreme. D personalities have to beware of their tendency to be inconsiderate, sarcastic, reckless, rude, **domineering,** proud, impatient, unemotional, conceited, ruthless, arrogant and offensive. They hear differently and see conflict as a challenge and an opportunity to speak their mind. They do not always mean to come across as inconsiderate in their quest to win. Their competitive nature just drives them to say and do what they feel. D personalities do not like to admit when they are wrong and they always like to be right. They see the bottom line and are impatient with those who do not get to the point quickly. D's will do something themselves if the job is not being done correctly. They do not like indecision, laziness, slow activities, slow people and slow talkers who don't produce. They hate taking orders and do not see the importance of stroking and complimenting people. When dealing with a D it is good to diplomatically offer advice, correction and direction. Under control D's can be great leaders who are courageous, **determined**, goal-directed, practical, productive and able to get the job done. When they temper their personality with love and patience, they can be very effective people. D's thrive in competition and are always going places. When they remember to bring people along in getting the job done, they become powerful leaders.

The next personality is the I. The I personalities are **outgoing and people oriented**. The I's are characteristically fun loving talkers who are happy-go-lucky. I's never meet a stranger and love to go places where there are a lot of people to talk to and have fun with. Their friendly personality is marked with enthusiasm and warmth. The I's can be **inspirational**, personable, **influencing, impulsive, illogical,** persuasive, excited, spontaneous, **interactive**, upbeat, humorous, happy. They thrive with many friends and relationships.

The strengths of a I personalities can also become their weaknesses if carried too far. I personalities can drive people crazy when they don't know when to shut up and listen. They wrongly believe that talking and doing is synonymous in terms of work. They are good starters but lack the focus and determination to see it through to the end. They are easily distracted and impulsive when out of control. I's need to guard against being unstable, undisciplined, unrealistic, manipulative, restless, emotional, loud, impulsive, undependable, unfocused, egocentric, excitable, exaggerative, purposeless, and nosey. They tend to put things off and do things at the last minute. I's can fly high in life but when they get low, they tend to go lower than normal. I's like to be around people and enjoy lots of activity. They are happy people who enjoy making others happy. They are the life of the party and are fun to watch. This is why they hate to be isolated, ignored or ridiculed. I's love recognition and approval. They are positive, upbeat people who like to stimulate others. I's are indeed the spices of life that offer us all a breath of fresh air.

The next personality style is the S. The S personality is reserved but loves to be around people. The S personality can be described as a **steady, stable and supportive** person who loves **stability** and **security**. They love to **support** and **serve** others in a **submissive** attitude. S's are **sentimental,** reserved, **shy,** relaxed and easygoing.

The strengths of an S can also be pushed to a weakness. The S personality must guard against being timid, **shy,** unmotivated, **self-**

protective, indecisive, uncommunicative, inflexible, reluctant, resistant to change, resentful, poor starters and from being easily manipulated. S's do not like to be yelled at, misunderstood, surprised, pushed or made fun of. They thrive in friendly environments where things are stable. They work well with others and have a team spirit. They have a stabilizing and peaceful effect on people. However, if you push them into a corner they will let you have it in the end. They can take a lot but when you cross the line they can be explosive. S types are motivated by helping others and are seldom in a hurry. They need lots of appreciation and will support and defend those they are connected to. While they may be indecisive and reluctant they are the most loyal people who will follow through and finish whatever they commit to. S personalities are nice people who want everybody and everything to be peaceful and calm. They aim to please and are indeed the peacemakers of the world.

The next personality style is the C. C Personalities are task oriented and reserved. C personalities are careful and **cautious** in their approach to life. They are characteristically **competent** people who like to be right and **correct**. They look at the details and **conform** to the rules. They're cognitive skills enable them analyze and **calculate** things in a very logical manner. C's like for things to be in order and in **compliance**. They like to know the facts and reasons behind information.

The C personalities can push their strengths to a weakness that can easily offend others. Their just the facts' attitude can cause them to come across as **cold** and uncaring of other people's feelings. They can become moody, **critical**, rigid, **compulsive**, impractical, unsociable, inflexible, worrisome, picky, and a perfectionist. C's may forget the spirit of the law as they attempt to enforce the letter of the law. This can cause them to never be satisfied. C's want **conformity** but cannot stand to be corrected or criticized. Sudden changes and unnecessary interruptions can cause them to be irritable. C's need quality answers and organization in their life to satisfy their need for order. They will always see to it that things are being done in a **correct** manner. Their meticulous style and **consistency** can insure that things go the way they have been planned and set up.

Now that we have defined the four basic styles and personalities of the **DISC model**, you may have already discovered your basic approach to life. You may see that you have some of the other traits in all four styles. Research has discovered that about 80% of all people are a blend of two and sometimes three personality styles. However, there is always a dominant style that is in primary control of the two to three secondary styles. As the secondary styles serve the primary style, they form a blended personality that makes up the total style of your personality. Sometimes these styles complement each other and sometimes they may cause conflict. The point in discovering this is so you can identify your strengths and weaknesses and then improve your people skills and personality. There is no right or wrong personality style, and there is no preferred style. We are all different and the DISC model provides a tool that helps us to understand and appreciate our differences in life. We all have value and we all have something to contribute to society. **Understanding this alone can revolutionize your ability to communicate and understand others.**

Chapter Three

Family Life

In this chapter we will be discussing **the importance of the family** and the roles husbands and wives should have to create a home that is full of love and peace. After we address the traditional family between a man and a woman, we will address the non-traditional family and the issues of sex and sexuality. It is of great importance for both traditional and non-traditional families to respect one another and realize that we live in a day where there are multiple views and options that are being practiced in today's society. I would like to stress that in a pluralistic world there has to be respect for all who sincerely desire to live a life filled with beauty and love. In this spirit, I believe we can live and let live if we realize that everyone is unique and different. As long as we all live our life from the law of love, we can live at peace, one with another!

Family life is one of the most important parts of our existence. The traditional family is the basic, grass root creation of God and the Universe. God created male and female in His image and together they reflect the attributes of God. God is neither male nor female. He is God. He possesses both male and female characteristics. In the creation of male and female, He chose to create two beings that could draw together as one and enjoy each other as they ruled the earth. This union between male and female is a sacred bond that Jesus referred to when He described His relationship with the church. Therefore, in most religions, the family unit is the cornerstone of God's creation. It is the most important thing in life next to our relationship with God. Anything that takes priority over the family was not considered good or healthy. When our homes and families are out of order, our lives will pay the consequences. Therefore, we must have a well-balanced family life that exemplifies the character of God.

The husband-wife relationship is the cornerstone of the family unit. According to the bible, when God created man He discovered that it was not good for man to be without a helpmate and companion. So He created a woman to stand beside the man to rule the earth. A man was to leave his family and find a mate to establish a new family to continue the process of multiplying and ruling the earth. The two would unite in marriage and become one flesh. Together they would reflect image of God and together rule the earth. The husband and wife were designed by God to rule the earth as male and female reflections of Himself. Our mission in marriage should be to expand the image of God in all we do! This principle has been upheld, for the most part, in all of the world's cultures to some degree or another.

A husband should love his wife, cherish her, take care of her and enable her to grow and flourish. He should allow her to blossom, grow and expand as the female image of God! If she is not blossoming like a beautiful flower then he needs to take responsibility to see to it that she does. He should care for her physically, mentally, financially, emotionally, spiritually and in every way. He needs to love her and let her be the blessing to she was created to be for him, their family, and the world! Women represent the feminine, nurturing character of God. When they are free to blossom, they nurture us all!

As fathers, men should raise their children to respect God and all of His creation, and they should teach them and instruct them by example. They should listen to their children, love them, and discipline them with the goal of helping them become better. Fathers should shape their children's personalities and channel their energies in a positive way. They should encourage them and never provoke them to anger and frustration. It is a father's responsibility to help his children and shape them to use their talents and gifts in their own unique way. Remember that they need love and affection more than advice. Show them what a loving husband and father is. Demonstrate to them what it means to be a wonderful person by being a living example to follow.

A wife should treat her husband with respect and honor. She should treat him the way she wants him to be and encourage him. A nagging wife is like dripping faucet and Chinese torture. She should spend time building her husband up and rise with him. She should never put him down or talk negative about him, especially around her family and friends. A wife who is also a mother, should teach her children, instruct, discipline, and guide them. She can shape their wills but allow them to be who they are. No two children are alike and everyone is different in their general make-up. She should learn to encourage her children and give them room to grow. She should give her children enough rope so they can get rope burns, but not enough to hang themselves. Our job, as parents, is to raise children up and let them go. They ultimately belong to God and the universe and we are at best surrogate parents for God's children. Therefore, we must raise them for God and the universe and not for ourselves.

Wives and husbands should dress nice and look their best for each other. Keep the romance in your marriage. Keep the fires stoked. Rekindle the fire of love by being an attractive mate inside and out. It is healthy and will keep a marriage going. Love each other and care for each other in every way. Remember that your actions will speak louder than words. When you live a wonderful life before your spouse, he or she will begin to see your inner beauty that is reflected spiritually, emotionally, physically and in your overall presence. This will do more than any nagging or criticizing remarks and actions will accomplish.

Husbands need to remember that women need foreplay and emotional support. Wives need to hear the words 'I love you' often. Wine and dine her. Help her around the house. The more you do to help her, the better your love life will be in and out of the bed. Sex is more than a biological function. Sex is a gift from God for a man and woman to express their love for one another. It is the holy union of a man and woman that draws them together spiritually, physically, emotionally and mentally. True lovemaking happens in and out of the bedroom. So love each other and you will find that it has great rewards for your marriage.

A marriage requires work and there are countless resources available today that can help and assist you in your family life. Take advantage of these resources and work at making your marriage and home a loving environment. Your marriage, family and home life should be one of joy. Fulfilling your destiny means being the very best family member in your home. What are some things you would like to do for your spouse or family members? How can you improve? Do you need to make some apologies? Do you need to mend some fences? Do you need to tell someone you love him or her? Make your wrongs right and develop a plan to begin the process of becoming an awesome man or woman. Whenever you are wrong, admit it. When you are right, refrain from saying 'I told you so.'

A good marriage and home will be filled with love. Tell your family you love them. Show them through your actions, reactions and with your words. Husbands and wives should hold hands, cuddle and enjoy a healthy sex life. Compliment each other and share thoughts and feelings in a constructive way. Learn to communicate and confide in each other. Be patient and kind. Create time together and time alone. Eliminate all negative tones, bad vibes and faces. Control your anger and never yell, scream or shout at each other. True love will not judge or condemn. It will always look for the good and overlook the bad. Give off positive vibes and positive tones that build up your family. Marriage, the home and the family are the foundational building blocks of society.

In regards to all of this, it is necessary to address the issues of **sexuality** that are a part of everyone's life. Sex and sexuality preferences are a heated topic these days as the break-up of homes and families, single parenting and domestic partnerships have emerged as part of the family community. As a society these issues have to be addressed in order to produce a beautiful environment for all of God's people to not just survive, but thrive! As a former Christian minister I understand the emotions that run deep on all sides of this delicate issue. In my journey I discovered that much of what religious people believe and teach from the bible about sex is misinterpreted. Therefore, I believe that it is appropriate to share what the bible really says and does not say regarding sex!

You may or may not agree! But empowered people are not offended or threatened by an opposing view. This is where love and tolerance come in our attempt to live at peace with all people who are living out their life according to their convictions. I believe it is imperative that we **separate sex from religious tradition**. The scriptures are filled with sex stories and sexual adventures of all type. In the beginning we are taught we were born naked and stayed naked until the fall of Adam and Eve! So, according to the scriptures, we should be living a perfect life in a nudist colony with no shame or guilt! Later, men had multiple wives and concubines. Solomon wrote a whole book on sexual attraction that included graphic sexual innuendos and the account of two lovers getting to know each other. Sexual attraction, sexual arousal, and sexual behavior are a legitimate part of life! IT is what makes the world stay populated and what brings so much pleasure. In the Bible, David danced naked before the people of Israel! The bible is full of such stories and confirms the sexuality of all people is real and is an important part in life!

The act of sex in and of itself is a neutral biological act. Sex in and of itself is not wrong or dirty as some would have us to believe. Sex is the reproductive energy of the universe that creates life and sustains the reproduction of all of life! I do not believe that it is a sin to have sexual urges and sexual feelings. After all, this is the way we were created! This is why it is normal for boys and men to have erections while seeing a beautiful girl or woman. Truly, we cannot say that sexual arousal is dirty or wrong if God made us this way! We are sexual beings with a born natural curiosity to learn about sex and sexuality. So at what point in our curiosity does sex become immoral? Is all sexual exploration outside of marriage wrong? If so, then we are doomed! So who are we to believe?

Social standards can change from culture to culture. Religious dogma is different in a myriad of ways. Cultural and religious standards are a part of our world. However, **cultural and religious standards** are not always right and are subject to change. Not many people like to address these issues. But in our journey to live a life of happiness, this topic has to be discussed. Why? Because liberating sex from religion and cultural mindsets is imperative. The basic act of sex is neither moral nor immoral. So, when is sex and sexuality immoral? It is immoral when it harms us individually and/or harms others in any way. **Destructive behavior** is immoral, not sexual behavior that is simply normal and part of learning and exploring about sex. It is only natural for us to examine our genitalia, and discover the pleasures of sex. It is only normal to want to touch other people in a sexual way. It is who we are. We are sexual beings with sexual urges. The only time these urges become immoral is when they inflict harm through destructive behavior. In fact, I believe the absolute law of life is the law of love! Love never demonstrates destructive behavior. Love is constructive. If you are a person of love, you can do no harm to another human being.

So what is sexual sin? What is fornication? What constitutes adultery? Is homosexuality a sin? These are all cultural and religious terminologies that have guided people for ages. Some claim that all sex outside of marriage is wrong. Polygamy, concubines, prostitutes and adultery have been a part of life since the very beginning. In fact, many of God's famous leaders were a part of this culture of sex and sexuality. God warned but never condemned any of God's servants for being polygamists or for having many concubines. Certainly they were having sex with multiple partners. The bible records these acts. It is also hard to deny that sex was going on in those places where hundreds of women were living together as concubines. Nothing was ever said to condemn this activity in the bible either! The patriarchs participated in these relationships and while some were condemned, many were not. So fornication and adultery had to be something else other than polygamy or having sex with concubines.

So what actually was adultery and fornication in the bible? Adultery in the bible is a word that most associate with sexual sin. The word adultery actually means 'to violate the rights of another on any basis.' Consensual sex was never a crime unless it violated another man or woman's spouse. Adultery was always when there was a violation of the marriage covenant that two people have agreed upon. To be married to your spouse specifically binds you in a covenant agreement to be bound together spiritually, physically, mentally, emotionally, financially, and in every way. Whenever either spouse abuses or misuses that covenant in any of those ways, it constitutes adultery. It had to do more with mutual respect and honor being violated in a relationship than the act itself.

Therefore, adultery was more about a broken covenant than a sexual sin. If a man or woman violated a man or woman's spouse, he was considered an adulterer. Adultery was associated with the violation of property rights attached to a man or woman's livelihood. This is why a person who is raped is not guilty of any crime! The person who is raped is a victim unless it is proven they willingly consented. An objective study of **fornication** links immoral behavior to harmful acts that violated other people and harmed them in any way. Rape, for instance, is the immoral behavior of forcing someone to do something they do not want to do. Incest would be taking advantage of a loved one and harming them sexually. That is why we have laws that protect children from pedophiles and from being prostituted by parents or family members. Fornication always involved harmful acts that violated another person's rights.

So what about homosexuality and lesbianism? Traditional, conservative religion repudiates alternative lifestyles. After all, it was Adam and Eve, not Adam and Steve according to religion! Yet, nontraditional religion has embraced alternative lifestyles as long as it is between two consenting adults who love each other. So what are we to believe and do about this dilemma? Should gay and lesbians be allowed to get married? In a pluralistic society, I believe that they should be able to live the lifestyle they choose and enter into a mutual, loving and respectful relationship. It is not the government or religious organization's right to disrespect that which is respectful. If they choose to enter into a relationship, then that should be their right as long as it does not harm or violate other people's rights. Whether we agree with the lifestyle or not, it is imperative we uphold the rights of others to live in peace in any way they so choose. This is why there should be legal civil unions for gay and lesbian people who are moral citizens in our society. Homosexuality is not what God hates. He is not a God of hate but a God of love. God expects us to live a life of love and when we operate in the law of love we are ethical and moral.

The sin of Sodom and Gomorrah in the Bible was the violation and disrespect of visiting guests by the mob who wanted to force them to have sex. In fact, everywhere Sodom and Gomorrah is mentioned, the sin of homosexuality is never mentioned, and it is the sin of disrespect! In the New Testament it was homosexuality associated with cultism that exploited women, men and children in sexual prostitution that was condemned. Again, adultery and fornication is the harmful act of hurting others and violating people's rights. Not consensual sex between two adults that are not violating anyone else's rights. Therefore, whether we are traditional or non-traditional, respect for loving relationships in a pluralistic society should be honored.

The last sexual topic we will address is **Nudity**. Is nudity and nude art evil? If writing about sex is porn then the bible is a pornographic book! Writing about sex is not sinful. Nudity and nude art are not immoral unless they involve the violation of another person's rights and/or depicts that which is harmful and immoral. So what is immoral? Forcing someone to do something they do not want to do, violating the rights of others and taking advantage of the vulnerable. Yes, much of the porn industry is disgusting and immoral, but sex can be beautiful if presented in a healthy way. Anything can be abused and can lead to immoral behavior, but sex in the Arts is not immoral. Go back in history and you will find nudity and sexual art as a normal part of life. After all, we would all be walking around naked if we believe the biblical account of Adam and Eve!

At this point, I would like to encourage everyone to live life and respect the way other people live their lives. I believe the guiding principle of love is sufficient for us all to accept and respect other people's lifestyles. As long as no one is being abused, harmed, or violated, we must all learn to tolerate all loving lifestyles. Whether we are traditional or progressive in our beliefs, we need to learn to live and let live as we love and extend love to all who desire to live a loving life of respect.

As we conclude this chapter I would like to share some parenting skills as they relate to raising positive children in a challenging world. Parents have the duty and responsibility to nurture, teach, train, and instruct children diligently as they provide for them spiritually, mentally and physically through positive support and encouragement. Children are to be controlled and corrected in a merciful and sympathetic way as we encourage them to embrace their uniqueness and worthiness.

The Recovery of Discipline is essential in today's world. Parenting is a great responsibility that must not be taken lightly. True discipline is the process of educating, instructing, cultivating and improving our children by giving them comprehensive instruction in the arts, sciences, correct sentiments, morals, and manners with due subordination and respect to authority. Discipline is also the act of instructing, educating, governing, teaching and informing the mind. Discipline can require punishment that is corrective rather than punitive. Corrective punishment should always be helpful to the child to recognize the problem, reconcile the problem and resolve the problem the child is experiencing. Corrective punishment should be done in an atmosphere of love, respect, and dignity. The focus should always be on finding solutions and not establishing blame.

In the process of discipline children should be able to communicate their feelings and feel as if they have been listened to. All consequences should be a learning experience enforced in a respectful and reasonable way. When corrective discipline becomes a battle or war, we resort to anger, revenge, uncontrolled spanking, yelling, arguing and negative comments. This in return fosters resentment, revenge and retreat in children. No child should be struck or beaten. Light spanking is effective in small children who are not capable of understanding and comprehending instruction. But spanking should never be done when we are angry or upset. It should not bruise the child or leave whelps and broken skin or bones. Spanking is for correction not abuse! Be cool, calm and collective when you do it and don't scare the child into submission.

Parents should consider the child's motives and handle each situation accordingly. Willful disobedience should be handled differently from accidents, misjudgments and other outside influences. Cruel and unusual punishment should never be used. The deprivation of food, water and toilet facilities should not be used as corrective punishment. Deprivation of spiritual opportunities and family affairs should not be used as forms of restrictions and punishment. Be reasonable and remember that one week can seem like a year to a child. Think before you say stupid things. And if you do or say something stupid, be big enough to apologize and start all over. Your child will respect you more for admitting when you are wrong and have made a mistake.

When laying down the law of the land always remembers the spirit of the law so that you can readjust if you need to. The biggest parental mistakes are strictness, permissiveness, pampering, spoiling, false threats, false promises and unreasonable limits of discipline. Establish responsibilities and privileges around the house. Set reasonable limits with logical consequences. Ask children to accept your limitations. Make them learn to communicate and talk in a reasonable fashion. Learn to communicate and dialogue with your children so that you are not always confronting and correcting them. You need to be in a relationship with them that is friendly, not adversarial. Children need to feel that they are capable, significant, influential, disciplined, responsible and able to communicate and make good choices. Give them the chance to make mistakes in a safe environment. Give them enough rope to get rope burns but not enough to hang themselves. Be firm when necessary but show respect. Children need parents more than they need a friend. Stay in your place and help them mature and grow. The next few principles I discovered through my experience of being a parent, a professional childcare worker, and a minister. Here is some positive **Principles of Discipline** for parents and guardians of children.

The process of Discipline should give a child two choices or more when you are making decisions concerning their life. This helps them feel as if they have a choice and are part of the process. This will help and encourage compliance and future success. Model the behaviors you want. Show the child by example how you want them to behave. Children imitate and reflect their parents! Think before you place a child in a situation that they are unable to handle. Prepare them and thereby protect them from failure. Children can overcome a lot if they are informed and given the opportunity to accept responsibility. However, if they are thrust into situations without proper training they are being set up to fail. Always remember, responsibility requires accountability. Do not bail a child out of trouble but use it to teach them right and wrong. There are consequences to the choices we make in life and children need to experience both failure and winning. Life is full of ups and downs. It's what we do with failure that makes us better or worse. So capitalize on failure to teach the importance of failing forward. A set back is an opportunity for the child to make a comeback!

When in the heat of a problem, learn to discuss things later when everyone has a chance to cool off and think things through. You do not have to make a decision immediately. Sometimes it is better to wait before doing things we will regret later on. Give encouragement as often as possible. Children need to be complimented and told often that they are made in the image of God and that they have great potential. Reward them with your encouragement and loving comments that promote a healthy self-image. Speak good things over your children and concentrate on their strengths. Never embarrass a child in front of others, especially their peers. Always move to a private place to talk when you have a problem to correct or address.

Children need to know that respect is one of the most important and natural responsibilities we have in living a successful life. Respect is essential to living a wonderful life. Respect for God, authority, the elderly, parents, family relationships, friends, peers, property, nature, and last but not least, respect for self are of the utmost importance.

Parents, you should provide an environment where your children can grow and mature into their unique self. You have an awesome responsibility to raise your children since they are on loan to you until they grow up and continue the process expanding and reflecting the good of God and the Universe! Once they leave home, they are released from your responsibility. But until then, you must fulfill your responsibility to raise your children and delegate that responsibility to someone else. Your church, school and caregivers can help you, but you are the one who is responsible. Raising positive children in a negative world can be and must be done. So stop making excuses and do it! You can change the world, and you can start by raising children to go out and change the world.

Chapter Four

Physical Life

Everyone, I believe, would like to live longer and live younger. There are some basic realities we need to recognize for living a life of health, energy, and vitality. **First,** we need to get back to the basics of life and realize that in our modern, high-tech world of food manufacturing; health and nutrition have been set aside and sacrificed for convenience and profit. Food manufacturers and the FDA look after the safety of our food only from the stand point of protecting us from eating food that will immediately make us sick. The long term effects are ignored and that is why you see so many drugs and other substances banned long after they have been approved by the FDA. This proves that they are not as concerned over your health as you may think! You have to take responsibility for your own health because no one else can or will. Doctors, for the most part, only prescribe drugs for symptoms and rarely address the causes. Our modern day health care crisis is a symptom of the sad American diet (the 'sad' diet) and lifestyle. The majority of our health care problems are due to people abusing their bodies and not taking care of them!

Second, in spite of our modern, space-age, high-tech medical community, sickness and diseases continue to rise in our world! Diseases are now showing up in young people that once only showed up in older people. People may be living longer, but is living in a wheelchair, a hospital bed or a nursing home really living? All the rates of disease are increasing as well as the costs to manage them. People are demanding health care reform without demanding lifestyle reform. Everyone should have access to a good health care education along-side a good medical health care plan! As Americans and citizens of the world, we should insist that we are properly educated, informed and provided **the keys** to live an optimum life of health and energy

Key One: Eliminate adulterated food. Any food source that has been adulterated by the manufacturing process is no longer a viable food source. Before the invention of manufacturing plants, people survived by purchasing fresh fruits, vegetables, and grains from local farmers and community mills. They did not use the modern manufacturing technologies that allow food to be shipped and stored for long periods of time. If food was stored, it was done so by more natural means. No form of food preservation is perfect but foods found on the shelves of grocery stores are more chemical than food. The preserved foods to avoid the most are as follows:

1. **White Sugar**: Processed sugar cane is white and has no nutritional value at all. It comes in many forms such as white table sugar, fructose, sucrose, high fructose corn syrup, corn syrup, and many other chemical names. White sugar provides no nutrition to the body and ultimately turns to fat! It weakens the immune system and causes blood sugar problems that lead to diabetes, high blood pressure, cholesterol, stroke, heart disease, and cancer. Use raw, unfiltered sugar and raw honey sparingly. Try Stevia for a natural sweetener that can be used in beverages, etc. And remember, sugar hides in every food made today from sodas to ketchup. Do not use **Aspartame or artificial sweeteners!**

2. **White Flour**: White flour is the result of manufacturers stripping all the good nutrition from the grain and leaving only a chemical

powder that is void of all nutritional value. This is why they have to add artificial vitamins and minerals and label it enriched! But it is not enriched with good nutrition; it is enriched with cheap, artificial vitamins and minerals that are not healthy for you! This product has no nutritional value and it has been proven that you would eventually die if this is all you ever ate. It has no fiber, no food value and will create a toxic waste of gunk that will clog up your intestines and arteries and will make you fat! It will do just as sugar does. It will kill you over a long period time with overworking your digestive system and causing diabetes, heart disease, strokes, high blood pressure and all kinds of health challenges. This includes white rice which goes through a similar process. Eat whole grains that are organic and sprouted. Eat whole grain rice that is wild or brown. Eliminating white flour products and white rice will add years to your life and life to your years! Grains need to be eaten in their natural, uncooked state or they cause problems!

3. **White Salt:** White table salt is a killer! It is a toxic chemical that will cause high blood pressure, heart disease, stroke, bloating and weight gain. It will also make you fat and eventually kill you. Instead of using salt, use natural herbs for seasoning. If you must use a salt shaker use Celtic Sea Salt or some other raw, natural salt that is dark or pink in color like Himalayan salt.

4. **White Grease**: Stop the use of lard, fat back, margarine, and heated cooking oils that are hydrogenated. These oils will clog your body and make you fat! Natural oils that are raw, cold-pressed, virgin, extra-virgin and unprocessed are healthy and good for you. Your diet should contain a good balance of natural essential fatty acids that have not been processed by heat. Cook lightly with raw coconut oil and cold-pressed olive oil. Supplement your diet daily with organic essential fatty acids, especially the omega 3's.

5. **White Dairy**: Milk does not necessarily do a body good! In the good old days we got our milk straight from the cow. Today milk is pasteurized, homogenized and processed to death. There is little nutritional value in dairy and it is very mucous forming. Many

people can eliminate dairy from their diet and all their sinus, cold, allergy and congestion problems will go away! A healthy alternative to milk is almond milk and rice milk. If you can find raw dairy products or grass fed dairy products you may use them sparingly. Milk is not the greatest source of protein or calcium. Think about it, where did the cow get its protein? From eating grass and grains! Fermented and raw dairy is always the best.

6. **Fast Food**: America eats on the run and depends on fast food to live far more often than not. Doughnuts, pastries, hot dogs, hamburgers, French fries, sodas, battered foods, deep fried foods, potato chips, cookies, ice cream, desserts, white biscuits, white bread, pasta, noodles, over cooked vegetables, and all other fast food will eventually destroy your health as they fatten you up for the kill! Microwave food, pre-packaged food, processed food and processed meats and adulterated foods are not food! Slow down and take care of your body! Eliminate negative nutrition from your diet and I guarantee you will **feel better, look better and most importantly, live better and enjoy life to its fullest extent!**

Key Two: Eat healthy and live healthy! You can live a healthy lifestyle that is natural just as easy as living an unhealthy lifestyle. You learned how to live with an unhealthy lifestyle and now you can learn to live a healthy one, if your desire for health is greater than your weaknesses. Do you want to live better, look better and fell better? Then make up your mind now that you can change! Change is not always easy but you can do it! It is a choice between life and death. After it is made, you will wonder why it was so hard to change for the better! **The keys** to a healthy lifestyle that will make you look better, feel better, and live better are natural laws that work for everyone! Nature does not play favorites. Neither does God! If you will eliminate adulterated food and adopt a healthy lifestyle you can add years to your life and life to your years! The keys to this healthier life are as follows:

1. **Fresh Air and Sunshine**: Everybody needs to benefit from fresh air and sunshine. Air is the single most important nutrient we put into our body. Breathing fresh air is vitally important to sustaining

good health. Therefore, the more we can get outside and breathe fresh air or allow fresh air into our living environments, the better health we will have. Air purification systems are good but nothing beats fresh air!

In addition to fresh air, we need to be exposed to the sun for good health. I am not talking about burning yourself or getting overexposed to the sun. Too much of anything can be bad for you. However, God designed us to need sunlight. Sunlight is nutrition! Sunlight turns cholesterol into Vitamin D. It is healthy and part of an overall plan for good health. The sun does not cause cancer! Cancer cells cause cancer. If you have an unhealthy body that cannot fight off cancer cells then overexposure to the sun could enhance a problem already there. But the sun is not the villain, lifestyle is! The sun is an essential part of life. Without the rays of the sun, this world we live in would not survive. But remember, balance is the key.

2. **Rest and Sleep:** Your body needs adequate sleep and rest. If you allow yourself to get run down due to lack of rest and sleep, you will begin to experience bad health. During sleep, the body has an opportunity to regenerate itself and allow the brain and nervous system to reboot. Eating before bedtime keeps the body from resting properly as it has to divert energy to digestion rather than regeneration. The more consistent your sleeping patterns are, the better you will feel on a daily basis.

3. **Pure Water:** Water is the second most important nutrient your body needs. Your body is largely made of water and it is necessary to drink adequate amounts of water daily that is as pure as possible. The best source for water is in raw, sun ripened fruit. Fruit contains not only vitamins, minerals and other nutrients, but it also contains the best water we can put into our bodies. The next best source of water would be raw vegetable plants, and then water itself. Soft drinks, coffee and other man made drinks are not the best supply of water. Drink pure water and cook with pure water. Be sure that you have some type of water filtration device for your water supply. Most water supplies are contaminated with pollutants, chemicals and inorganic minerals.

4. **Exercise and Activity:** There are more than 600 muscles and 200 bones in the body that need to be exercised, as well as fluids that need to be properly circulated to maintain good health. In addition to that, the cells of our body need to be worked out in the process to aid in proper assimilation of nutrients and the elimination of waste and toxins. Our bodies were designed to be active and in motion. A sedentary lifestyle leads to a host of problems. Therefore, we must do some form of exercise that will assist the body to be healthy and strong!

5. **Food and Nutrition:** Healthy foods produce healthy bodies! Junk food produces unhealthy bodies. As we discussed in the first key, we must eliminate adulterated foods from our diet. In place of them should be foods that are wholesome and rich in vitamins, minerals, fats, and other unknown nutrients in natural foods. I recommend eating organic fruits and vegetables as much as possible and as close to the way God and nature made them. The use of preservatives, artificial colors, flavors, additives, stabilizers and chemicals are killing us slowly but surely.

So what dietary requirements determine ideal foods? Our foods should be as close to the way God and Mother Nature created them as possible if we expect to have superlative well being. Foods must be easily digested when eaten alone or when properly combined with other foods. Indigestion, bloating, heartburn, acid-reflux, bad breath and other digestion problems are signs of poor digestion and putrefaction in the body. Ideal foods will be rich in amino acids (protein), organic vitamins, minerals, good fats and other nutrients. Organically grown foods contain organic vitamins, minerals, fats and other nutrients that the body can use. If foods are grown and processed as close as possible to the way God made them, they will provide our bodies the necessary nutrients we need to live productive lives. Our foods should also be alkaline with respect to their metabolic reaction in the body. Foods that leave an acid base are hard to digest and putrefy in the intestines. This produces gas, body odor, contaminated body fluids (toxic mucus) and waste that render an unhealthy body. Over cooked food, processed food, junk food and improper food combining cause this unhealthy acid condition. The body was not designed by God to eat the types of food we consume today. Disease thrives in an acid body and cannot survive in an alkaline body.

Also, **food combining** is one of the most important things you must learn to insure that your body will properly digest, assimilate and eliminate food. If you abuse your body with improper food combining it will suffer the consequences sooner or later. You may think you are all right but you have a time bomb ticking in your body due to improper eating habits. Some foods are compatible and others are not. This is due to the fact that the stomach is not designed to digest a multiplicity of foods at one time. In the digestive process, proteins require a strong acid environment and carbohydrates require an alkaline (non-acid) environment. Carbohydrates need the alkaline saliva of the mouth and the alkaline juices of the intestine to complete digestion. Proteins activate the pepsin of the stomach, needed to break down the proteins (amino acids), and require hydrochloric acid for proper digestion. When you mix proteins and carbohydrates together they can neutralize each other so that neither types of food are properly digested, assimilated and eliminated. This can result in fermentation of the carbohydrates and acid by-products from protein that will spoil, rot and stink up the body. As we tax the digestion process in this manner we create a mess for the body to deal with.

So, what is the best way to combine and eat our foods? We will now consider all the major food groups and explain the best way to eat or not eat them with other foods. It must be noted that the best way to eat anything is by itself. Eating one thing at a time is always the best way to eat. The less the body has to deal with at one time the better. The combining of foods always causes the body to work overtime in the digestive process. However, there are some combinations that work fairly well and do not hurt the body in a critical way. So let's look at the best ways to eat our foods.

Fruits: The best way to eat any fruit is on an empty stomach all by itself. If you combine them at all remember to eat acid fruits with only acid fruits and sub-acid fruits with sub-acid fruits. When fruit is chewed well it is almost ready for immediate assimilation in the stomach. Fruit is by far the easiest food for the body to digest and eliminate. Fruits are the body's cleansers that strengthen the immune system.

Vegetables: Vegetables can be eaten with vegetables. However, only one or two cooked vegetables should be eaten with a combination of raw vegetables. The less cooked food you eat the better off you will be. Learn to lightly stir fry your vegetables in unprocessed oils or lightly steam them. Boiling, deep-frying and/or overcooking your vegetables destroy them and they become dead, devitalized foods. Never combine vegetables with fruit unless they are dark green vegetables. Vegetables can be eaten with the other food groups as recommended. Vegetables are your body's builders that strengthen the overall performance of the body.

Meat: Eat meat that is organically produced and free of growth hormones, steroids, antibiotics and chemicals used to enhance the profit margins of business. Meat should only be eaten with a raw salad and one to two cooked green vegetables. No bread, potatoes, starches, fruit, nuts, seeds or grains should ever be eaten with meat if you desire optimum digestion and assimilation.

Dairy: Limit dairy products if your dairy products are refined, processed, fortified, pasteurized, and homogenized as these processes turn dairy products into inorganic substances that are dangerous to the body. If you choose to eat dairy products, eat organic dairy products and raw unpasteurized dairy when you can. Only dark green vegetables should be eaten with dairy for optimum digestion.

Starches: Starches such as bread, pasta, potatoes, rice, beans and the like should never be combined with other starches. Eat one starch at a time with a raw salad and with no more than one to two cooked green vegetables. Never eat starches with fruit, meat, dairy, seeds or nuts.

Raw nuts and seeds: Eat each kind alone. Do not mix them together in any combination because they are hard to digest. In fact, they are easier to digest if soaked in purified water over night. They may be added to a raw salad with one or two cooked green vegetables. Never eat them with fruit, meat and dairy products.

Dried fruits: Eat each kind alone that are organic and have no sulfur or sugar added to them.

Fats: Unprocessed, virgin, cold pressed or first pressed oils are best eaten with raw salads or taken on an empty stomach. If you cook with them, use them sparingly.

Digestive Enzymes: If you eat cooked food or combine foods in wrong combinations, then digestive enzymes should be taken with meals. They will aid the body to digest your foods due to the fact that your digestive system has been overloaded as it tries to digest, assimilate and eliminate your wrong combination of foods. Foods that are eaten alone require the following digestion time. Fruit requires thirty minutes, and vegetables require one hour. Seeds, nuts and grains require two to three hours. Fish requires 2 hours. Chicken and turkey require two to three hours. Veal and lamb require three to four hours. Beef requires five hours and pork requires seven or more hours to leave the stomach. Drinking with a meal or adding other kinds of food can double or triple the amount of time to digest your food!

6. **Insure your Health with Whole Food Supplements.** Not all supplements are created equal! Most of what is on the market today is synthetic and/or produced with sub-standard raw materials that can be contaminated and dangerous to your health. The right kind of food supplement can insure that you are getting everything you need nutritionally to keep you healthy. No one eats enough of the right kind of foods all the time. Therefore it is imperative that we add safe, organic, whole food supplements to our diet!

7. **Have an Attitude of Gratitude!** A sound body requires a sound mind! Good health revolves around us keeping a positive attitude and resisting all negativity in our life. Negativity of any type is a breeding ground for disease. Negative emotions and attitudes have been proven to cause all kinds of illness in our lives. Learn to laugh at life and be happy! Happiness is like medicine that can assist us to heal all of our ills: mentally and physically! Say your positive affirmations and live a life of happiness!!

8. Stay Persistent and Consistent. Make up your mind that you can be healthy and happy on the inside and out! Always keep on keeping on and never give up even if you have failed. Learn to fail forward! Those who stay persistent will eventually cross the finish line and win. Those who give up never make it. Don't give up! You can be healthy and happy. Don't let yourself or anybody else hold you back. Be strong and be bold.

Health is a state of soundness whereby the spirit, mind and body are in a state of harmony. In perfect health, the whole person will be operating the way God intended. Sickness and disease will not be a part of his life. When we experience disease, it is always body instituted and conducted for the purpose of cleansing, repair and restoration of health and vitality. Disease does not occur in people who are in harmony with God in their spirit, mind and body. Colds, flu bugs, allergies, viruses, bacterial infections, cancer and all disease are a result of being out of harmony with God in your spirit, mind or body. When harmony is achieved, all will be well. **Constructive disease** begins when the body has sufficient nerve energy to cause toxic waste to be eliminated. **Degenerative disease** occurs when the body is so toxic that all the cells, tissues, systems and other areas of the body have been broken down and crippled to the point that they are overtaxed and overworked yielding them ineffective to do their part to maintain health and vitality.

People self-destruct by unnatural lifestyles that corrupt their spirit, mind and body. The American diet and lifestyle are, according to government statistics, the top killers of Americans. These lifestyles cause heart disease, cancer, strokes and obstructions of the heart, accidents, pneumonia, diabetes, HIV, suicide and chronic liver disease. It is estimated that diet and lifestyle issues account for 90% of all deaths. Of that 90%, nutritional problems account for 76% of deaths. It is amazing to know that 90% of the causes of death could be eliminated if people would choose to practice common sense principles of health by nourishing their bodies with foods that are assimilated and eliminated properly.

In your journey you will need to take one thing at a time. You did not get in your condition overnight and you will not be healed overnight. Do not get overwhelmed with everything in the process of being transformed. Enjoy the journey. Take it one day at a time. Your desire to change will be honored by God. Do not allow yourself to fall under any condemnation along the way. Yes, you are in a battle and things will not always be easy, but do not be hard on yourself by making this a set of rules and regulations.

It is now time to makeover your life, refine your figure, and reenergize your life! No matter who you are or where you are in life, YOU absolutely and positively do have the power to Makeover your life! When you gain control of your body, you will gain control of your life! The body is the epicenter of your universe and you go nowhere in this life without IT. If your body is sagging, dragging, softening and aging rapidly, other aspects of your life will soon follow. Nobody sets out to be unhealthy. But sometimes, slowly and gradually, at some critical moment, without even being aware of it, many times, we give up and let go. In doing so, we in turn may give up on our health and ultimately give up on life.

When you feel unhealthy and unhappy about your body you lose self-confidence and acquire a poor self-image. When this happens, these feelings can lead to failure and frustrations in other areas of life. The body is part of our three-fold make-up: the body, the mind and the spirit. When the body is dragging us down, it is hard to be spiritually and emotionally healthy. Whenever we are ill spiritually, mentally or physically it affects us holistically. Therefore, it is imperative that we take control of the body as we discipline ourselves mentally and spiritually. Taking control of our lives will cause us to develop dreams, goals, incentives, challenges, opportunities and purpose. Purpose driven people are alive! Taking control of our lives helps us to develop magnetic personalities that can inspire others! Enlightened people enlighten others! Empowered people empower others! So decide today to take control of your body and revolutionize not only yourself but others.

Are you ready to jump the gap and cross over the abyss of fear, doubt, frustration, hopelessness, depression, cynicism, and disillusionment? There is a world of difference between knowing what to do and doing it! There is within each of us the desire to thrive, not just survive! Life is an obstacle course and strength comes from resistance training. Challenges are opportunities for us to overcome and learn more about life. Pressure or stress is the fuel for growth and is the antidote for breaking out of the muck and mire you may find yourself in. As we discover what we don't want, we can then move on to what we really do want. Embrace the passion of a winner by rising to every challenge to beat the obstacles of life and determine to never give up! And remember, we sometimes fail forward. So focus on the progress, not perfection.

So, **how do we jump the gap?** It all starts by looking deep inside for honest answers. We have to honestly look at who we are, where we are, what we are, and why we are where we are! Are you willing to look honestly at yourself and then honestly make the drastic changes and transformations to refine your life, reenergize your body, and revolutionize your life? It is time to stop making excuses and time to make a decision to makeover your life! **YOU can do IT!** The question is, will you? Now is the time to look deep inside and honestly assess your life. The following questions need to be answered honestly and with the anticipation that this is the beginning of a new life. It is not about judging and condemning but about discovery and refocusing your life for the better! When you look at yourself, do you honestly like what you see? How do you really feel about yourself? What are the pro's or con's of staying on the pathway you are on now? Would you like to create a brighter future? Do you really want to refine your figure, reenergize your life, and revolutionize your life? Are you willing to change? Why do you want to change? How important is this to you? Are you willing to give up some things to have what you want? When do you want this? Are you ready to plan, work the plan and stay the course no matter what?

Now it is time to write down your vision and develop a dream board. It is imperative that you write down what it is you desire to accomplish and find pictures from magazines, personal photos, brochures, or other media that you can put on a dream board, a refrigerator, a mirror, planner and other places that remind you of what you want to become. <u>**Write out your goals in detail**</u> and read them at least twice a day, in the morning when you first get up and right before bedtime. Read them out loud when you can with enthusiasm and with intense desire and faith that you will accomplish your makeover. Visualize your vision in your mind and on your dream board. What you visualize you will actualize! What you think about, dream about, and read about, you will become!

Discover and identify unauthorized negative patterns of action and identify new patterns of actions to overcome the negative actions. Transform the energy of adversity into positive energy. Challenges are opportunities to honor self promises to change and be true to yourself and your goals. The greater the battle, the greater the victory! Life, the ultimate challenge, is not a race to a finish line, but a process of continual growth. A plane expends more energy to lift it off than it does to sustain it in the air. This also applies to changing your life. If the plane gets off course, it has to apply more energy to get back on course. If you get off course, you will have to apply more energy to get back on course. Just remember that set backs are only opportunities to get back on track. If you stay persistent and consistent, you will prevail even with the setbacks that may come your way!

Transformation and change start within. Change is a part of life. It is just a matter of choosing to be in control of the change or allowing others to control your destiny. Control your life or others will control it for you! Be adaptive while you are proactive. Sometimes we have to change our methods while the goals remain the same. Learn how to adjust, adapt, react and change in a positive way. Whenever we become set in our methods and ways, we set ourselves up for failure. Change can be good if we recognize positive change and resist negative change. Intimate mind knowledge allows us to change when we need to. When you know what you want and where you are headed, you are empowered to choose life no matter what circumstances may challenge you. **Now is the time** to refine your figure, reenergize your life, and revolutionize your life. Don't wait another second to make over your life! It is time. You are ready. So just do it!

Now is the time to regain your life! When we are in the process of regaining our lives, we must realize that our transformation is a process that requires us to overcome the past patterns of life that have created who we are today. You can turn your life around in a positive way by renewing your life with proper nutrition for the spirit, mind, and body. As we release the past, we can create new changes that we deserve and achieve, as we let go of the past and reprogram our thinking. **The process** includes taking care of our bodies with good nutrition. It includes developing our spirit with prayer, meditation and a connection to God. The mind needs to be reprogrammed and renewed. It all works together for our good or for our defeat. What we think, what we say, what we do, and how we do it makes us who we are. When we decide to take full responsibility for our life and where it is today, we can begin a new life of total health and vitality!

Are you willing to release the past? Are you willing to replace those past patterns in life that have gotten you where you are today? Are you willing to embrace the fact that God loves you and wants the very best for you in every way? Do you want to experience a life of love, joy, peace, goodness, beauty and vitality? If so, you need to let go of all your past anger towards yourself and others. You must learn to forgive and be forgiven. **Let me ask you something?** Are you impatient, irritated, or frustrated, in any way? Do you have a critical spirit? Do you harbor resentment, jealousy or bitterness? If so, then release it now! Forgive yourself and forgive all who are making you feel this way, even if you feel they deserve to be criticized or scorned. Let it go! Ask for forgiveness from those you have agitated and release these deadly agitations right now!

Let me ask you again? Are you full of tension, anxiety, nervousness, worry, doubt, insecurity, feelings of rejection, unworthiness or fear? If so, release them and let them go! If you relate to any of this negative garbage, then you need to release these thoughts and patterns in your life. These are all thoughts that create disease in the body and cause us to be overweight, tired and run down. As we release these negative patterns in our lives we will begin to get healthy in every way. As we nourish our bodies with positive, life affirming foods, attitudes, and positive actions of love, peace and joy, we will live younger and longer! Learn to accept who you are, but remember that you can improve your life! Learn to love yourself and others in a healthy way and you will be healthy!

In addition to the principles of living a healthy life, I want to include information on the three distinct categories of human **body**

types: the endomorph, the mesomorph, and the ectomorph. Your body type, make up, and metabolism determine your tendencies to lose or gain weight. Your blood type can also affect your ability to gain or lose weight but more often than not, your body type affects the kind of diet and exercise program you should be on. Not everyone has the same kind of body and it is unrealistic to have expectations that you can look like a model or movie star. You must embrace and accept your body the way God made it. However, you can take care of your body and give yourself the ability to be the best you can be in every way. I want you to look good and feel good inside and out! Most people are usually a combination of all body types with one dominate body type, as we are all unique individuals. So let's take a look at all the body types and discover who you are and how you should approach your general lifestyle guidelines.

Ectomorph Body: The Ectomorph body is generally thin with little body fat or muscle mass. I call these people the "Barney Fifes" of the world. Ectomorph bodies are naturally skinny, lean, and have fast metabolisms. They generally can eat anything and everything and never gain weight. However, they can eat themselves into ill health as they remain lean and skinny. In order for an ectomorph to gain weight and fill out they need to eat a calorie rich diet of unprocessed foods that are organic, natural, and wholesome. Refined foods should be avoided by all people, but the ectomorph needs to realize that even though they can eat refined, processed foods and not gain weight, these foods can destroy their health.

Ectomorph bodies should eat every two hours and emphasize protein and starchy carbohydrates. Higher fat foods like peanut butter, whole eggs, red meat, and beans should be eaten freely. Heavy weight training will help stimulate muscle growth if they desire to build muscle. Cardio and other aerobic activities should be kept a minimum to conserve calories. I recommend rebounding for all body types. Ten to fifteen minutes a day is all that one needs to be healthy and fit. When rebounding, an ectomorph may want to use light weights in the exercise program for general health. I believe in accepting your body the way it is and just following a healthy diet for your body type. Exercise and incorporate affirmations into your spiritual and mental life to live a healthy and fit life.

Mesomorph Body: The mesomorph body is what I call the natural muscleman who usually has a more balanced body with excellent muscle tone and structure. A mesomorph body tends to shape and tone more easily than all other body types. These folks will gain or lose weight very easily and can put on pure muscle mass easily. Most successful body builders have this body type. Mesomorph bodies tend to have large heads, broad shoulders and a narrow waist. They tend to have a muscular body with strong forearms and thighs. They are genetically gifted in this way and have good shoulder to waist ratios. They make people who gain weight easy or can't gain at all a little upset. However, we must all realize that there is no such thing as one perfect body type. All bodies are perfect when we properly take care of them!

Mesomorph body types should eat a well balanced diet of unprocessed protein, carbohydrates and fats. As with all body types; sweets, junk foods and refined foods should be avoided. Exercise should be well balanced and again rebounding is the perfect exercise for all body types. If one wants to become a body builder, this body has the most potential. However, body building is a full time effort that has to be kept up to maintain the mass and look of a body builder. That is why it is good to just be happy with being fit and living a well balanced lifestyle. It is unrealistic for anyone to think that being a fitness model of any type is normal!

Endomorph Body: An endomorph body is basically a bigger boned body with a more round body type. This body type has a slower metabolism that can store fat easily. An endomorph generally has a soft body that gains weight like a pear. They will have slim ankles and wrists that serve to accentuate the fatter parts. Their slower metabolism makes weight gain easy and weight loss difficult. They genetically tend to store fat and even while gaining muscle mass, they will look soft, not ripped.

The endomorph needs to focus more on low sugar fruit, vegetables and lean protein. Starches should be avoided, and as with all body types, they need to avoid refined foods. Fat intake should be kept low and calories need to be kept low also. Second helpings should be avoided along with late night snacks. Meals should be light and light snacks such as protein or fruit should be utilized between meals to control hunger. All refined sugars need to be eliminated and alcohol should be eliminated or controlled to once a week. When it comes to exercise, the endomorph needs to work out consistently to keep weight under control. Again rebounding is the perfect exercise and the most effective way to maintain a daily exercise routine. Exercising on an empty stomach is essential for this body type! The more active an endomorph is the better!

Blood Types: There is a lot of information on blood type diets that can help and assist people adjust their diet. For instance, **O** blood types tend to need more protein and/or meat. **A** blood types seem thrive on a vegetarian diet. **B** blood types tend to need a more balanced diet of protein, fruit, and vegetables. **AB** blood types are the most sensitive of all blood types and a need a more balanced diet devoid of simulative foods such as caffeine. Discovering your blood type can further help you adjust your diet until you find a good blend of food and exercise that makes you look and feel good inside and out!

Metabolic Types: Our metabolism can also determine our diet. As we have already discovered, ectomorph body types will naturally have a higher metabolic system that needs food, fuel and energy more often than all body types. People with ectomorph bodies need to eat more hearty and more often. If you wake up in the morning and you are not hungry, then you are most likely an endomorph body type. It is best for this type not to eat until they are hungry. Start the day off with water and then exercise to rev up the metabolism. Mesomorph bodies can go either way, and need to listen to their bodies. Most mesomorph bodies need a well balanced breakfast that is not too heavy and not to light.

Personality Types: Personality types affect more how we approach life than how we should eat. Different personality types can cause one to be consistent or inconsistent; organized or unorganized; serious or carefree; adaptive or reactive. Personalities may cause us to stay on task or off task; like change or resist change. You are a special, unique person who has the potential to live an optimal life of health. You can live without sickness, disease, and obesity. You can look good and feel good inside and out. You can live life to its fullest extent. You were designed for abundance and I believe the best is yet to come for you!

In conclusion to this chapter, we are ending this chapter with the difference between **Health Care and Medical Care.** The art and science of Medical Care is rooted in Natural Health Care (Hypocrites) but has progressed into a crisis, disease and accident care system. The Medical Profession takes a symptomatic approach to relieve people of the symptoms of their problems for the most part through drugs and surgery. We have all experienced the magic of drugs and surgery. It is always a comforting thing to know that we have trained medical people to assist us in the care of ourselves and loved ones. I appreciate what doctors and medical people have done to help me and my loved ones. It is always good to have them around when you need them!

But in spite of our modern, high-tech, space-age health care system, sickness, disease and obesity are at an all time high! Why is this so? Is it because we don't have health insurance? NO! It is all lifestyle related! I believe that 95% of all health care problems are lifestyle related! People are demanding **Health Care Reform without Lifestyle Reform!** What we need is a health revolution that insists that we should be properly educated, informed, and provided the keys to living a healthy, fit life free from sickness and disease! The art and science of true Health Care addresses the overall constitution and makeup a person.

Disease happens when we are not at ease and our ability to cope with life and our environmental factors is compromised. The root causes of all disease are environmental stresses that overwhelm the body due to trauma, toxicity, and stress. **Trauma** creates stress induced from mechanical injury. Sometimes we get hurt in life through all kinds of injuries we sustain through sports, accidents, etc. **Toxicity** in our bodies is the result of accumulated poisons that the body can no longer eliminate properly. As a result, disease sets in. What we eat, drink, breathe, touch and come in contact with in life can pollute our physical bodies and overwhelm them with toxicity. **Mental, Emotional, & Spiritual Toxicity** can be created from stressful work, relationships, money challenges, religious conflict, and emotional conflicts. Stress from life can break down our ability to cope in every way.

Once we identify the cause of our disease, we can treat the cause. In doing so, we eliminate the symptoms. **Medical Care** treats the symptoms. **Health Care** treats the cause. Whenever we eliminate the environmental stresses, we return to overall balance constitutionally. Whenever one aspect of our constitution is out of balance due to stress, we get out of balance constitutionally. This is why disease needs to be approached holistically! The holistic approach is as simple as recognizing the **A, B, C & D's of Health.**

A is for Activate. Believe and trust in the body's ability to heal itself. God made a wonderful body that can heal itself if you give it the proper tools. Stimulate the healing process with positive affirmations and attitudes. What we believe and what we speak, affects who we are. Identify and address unresolved emotional conflicts. Use whole food supplements to balance the energies of the body. Most people are nutritionally deficient and need whole food supplementation. Do not think that fragmented, synthetic vitamins are good for you. Pray and meditate to attune to God, yourself and the Universe. Then make a conscious decision to choose life and reject sickness and disease.

B is for Build. Eat a well balanced diet of whole foods that are natural and unprocessed. Supplement with enzymes and probiotics along with your whole food supplements. Eat according to your constitution. Find out your body type and eat accordingly! Exercise smart, sleep soundly, drink pure water, & get some fresh air & sunshine!

C is for Cleanse: Drink pure water every day. Do 2-4 maintenance cleanses a year. Make sure you have 1-2 good bowel movements a day! Eliminate stress from your life! Change jobs, friends, family, churches, etc. if you need to! If you have a chronic disease that is life threatening you need to refrain from work, exercise, and all stress while you rebuild.

D is for Direct Aid. Identify constitutional deficiencies that need support through specific herbs, etc. Herbal and homeopathic formulations can assist our spirit, mind and body to heal and balance. Strengthening weak systems can help the body to rebuild from a weakened condition. The key is finding the root cause and not treating just a symptom. Seek out help through therapeutic services such as massage, physical therapy, chiropractic care, acupuncture, Rolfing, colonics, etc.

In addition to the A, B, C, and D's of holistic health, is belief in the body's ability to heal itself! The process of healing includes the belief in the Spiritual Forces of God to heal. Do not panic or be filled with fear. Negative thoughts are destructive and agitations of any type are deadly. Healing requires positive, healing thoughts. God uses natural laws and spiritual laws to heal. We must do our part and God will do His!

Completely surrender yourself into the hands of God. Through prayer, meditation, devotional reading and spiritual fellowship we attune to the Divine power of God. It is important to keep harmony in all our relationships as disharmony and disease are akin.

Visualize yourself in perfect health! Let the picture of health sink deep into your spirit, mind and soul and they will send forth radiant health energy. Negative thoughts have to be terminated and replaced with positive, life-affirming thoughts! Anxiety, fear, tension, resentment, guilt, unforgiveness and any combination of negative agitations are deadly. These deadly agitations clog up our ability to attune with God. We must resist them and release them. Mental pain produces physical pain. Let go and embrace the love and peace of God!

During the first stages of healing, one must be still and know that God is with you and assisting you. Completely rest and relax into the hands of God. Wait on the Lord, be of good courage, and He shall strengthen you! Affirm that you can overcome and get through anything with God's help. In God we live and move and have our being! Embrace the love of God and realize that God is ever- loving and is always ready to receive you into His positive, healing energy. Forgive yourself and forgive as God has forgiven you!

Remember that anger is an emotion that always causes one to be irritable, tense, rigid, and uptight. Don't harbor or brood over the past, present or future. Pray and vent your frustrations to God or someone who understands you need to vent to release the anger. But always remember, to vent is to release the anger and allow the love of God to heal the fires of anger. Ask God to take away the anger and fill your heart and mind with only love, joy, peace, goodness, patience, forgiveness and the discipline to control your anger.

Alter your life by altering your attitude. Only speak hopefully and positively about everything. Resist negativity of all kinds and do not use critical words towards yourself and others. Think on good things and refuse to entertain negative thoughts and imaginations that more than likely are just that, the imagination!

Learn to be yourself! Never allow your thoughts to become depressed or morbid. Engage in some form of activity that will allow you to express your better self. Live the lives God gave you and realize you are ample and complete. Live, love and laugh! Let your heart be glad and free!

Learn to love your work and give yourself to it. Service and giving to others in all love is the key to happiness! If you hate your job or work, change careers! Deep inside of every act of man is some form of desire to express. It is the Divine Urge within us all. People who are constantly being irritated have suppressed some desire to speak their mind. Anger, malice, vindictiveness and kindred emotions are but subtle forms of fear arising from a sense of inferiority. Congested emotions have to be released so that the creativity of our spirit can give birth to an expressive life.

There is always a connection to our overall health based on what is going on constitutionally with us spiritually, mentally, and physically. All the choices we make in these three areas affect who we are and our experiences in life. The cause of all sickness, disease, problems, and ill circumstances are rooted in our spirit, mind, and body. **What you sow is what you reap!** This is a universal law which simply says that what we think, say and do has good or bad consequences. What we feed ourselves spiritually, mentally, and physically affects who we are in every way. No one else is to blame.

We are personally responsible for who we are and where we are in life. God and the universe set this law up to assist us and support us in our quest for living a successful life. This is what I believe the sacred scriptures truly teach about judgment. We are living out the consequences of our own actions! If you are always blaming people and circumstances for your present state of life, then you are not living. You are surviving rather than thriving! This is good news! Why? Because, once we wake up to this fact, we realize if we change our present spiritual, mental, and physical actions we can change our life for the better!

This handbook has thus far encouraged you to awaken to the fact that you are born to succeed and live a wonderful life filled with love, peace, and joy! If you are still reading and studying this handbook, then you are learning how to change and live life to its fullest extent. Change is not easy. Changing our beliefs about life can be very challenging but also very rewarding.

At this point you should be ready to release the past and appreciate the past by learning from it and moving forward. Forgiving yourself and others of all hurt and harm is essential to moving forward. It is imperative that you release self-hatred, guilt, bitterness, fear, resentment, anger, impatience, frustration, jealousy, and criticism from your life and towards others. Release the past, forgive the past of all wrong doing, and accept who you are right now. As you learn to love yourself, approve of yourself, accept yourself and do likewise to others, you will be amazed how this will free you up to live! You can start all over new and fresh! **What you have created can be re-created!**

Health Affirmations are a part of the process of being healthy and staying healthy. The key to affirmations working is reading these affirmations out loud and with enthusiasm when you first rise in the morning and before you retire at night. The more you repeat these words the more they will transform you, especially when you feel tempted to give in to defeat. Start with these and then develop your own!

I affirm that I am a perfect, whole and complete person whose entire spirit, mind, and body is fit and fully functional on all levels. I am growing younger as I grow older and I look and feel healthy. Youthfulness flows through my body like electricity and all faculties are increasing. I choose to be active, happy and energetic.

I take full responsibility for my health and all my experiences. Therefore, I release all resentment, anger, criticism and guilt of myself and others. I release my failures and the failures of others. I am forgiven and I forgive others freely as God has forgiven me. I love my enemies and pray for those who come against me in any way.

I am a worthy person created by God to live a life of love, joy, peace, goodness, and beauty! I love myself and accept myself the way I am. However, I take full responsibility for the life I have and make positive choices that promote my overall health and vitality. I choose to fail forward and see setbacks as opportunities to learn and grow. I am steadfast and unmovable and I never give up on myself or others. I see the potential of a wonderful life in myself and in others. Every day is a new day and I live each moment as if it were my last. I release the past and I choose to move forward in a positive way.

Today is the first day of my new life, and I believe the universe is conspiring to bless me in every way. I believe in myself because God believes in me. I believe in others because God believes in them. I trust God and have the faith to believe that all things work together for my good. God loves me and as a loving parent desires for me to be blessed in every area of my life.

I open myself up to God and trust in the Infinite Intelligence of God to guide and direct me into all wisdom and knowledge that enables me to live a productive, healthy, and meaningful life. I am willing to release old beliefs and the limitations they have had on me. I am a free thinker who is able to think for myself and trust in myself to make the right decisions. I listen to all, but reserve the right to judge all and choose what is best for me! I respect everyone's right, including my own, to live and make our own choices.

God is supporting every thought that I choose to think, believe and profess. God loves me and want all the desires of my heart to come to pass. I am loved and I share that love with all that I can. I choose life and I choose to be fit for life in every way. I am happy and I am free to be me!

I accept my body and the unique way God created me. I therefore choose to take care of it in a positive way. I have **a picture** in my mind of what I want my body to look like. I reject all negative thoughts about my body and give thanks for the wonderful body God gave me. I reject all criticism from myself and others about my body and only think about how wonderful my body is.

I release all negativity from my life and only think good things about myself and others. I see my potential and likewise see the potential in others!

I only put good things to eat in my body that promote good health, strength and energy. I drink lots of pure water and eat wholesome foods. I do not need to eat junk food that produces junk bodies. I enjoy healthy foods and look forward to eating fresh fruit and vegetables.

I am reshaping my body by taking good care of it by thinking positive thoughts, eating healthy foods, drinking pure water, exercising, and releasing all toxic thoughts and poisons from my spirit, mind, and body.

I give thanks for the gift of life and for the body God gave me. I am healthy and energetic. I feel good and look good inside and out!

I am living younger as I grow older. My entire body and all of its cells, organs, and systems are healthy, strong, vital and keeping me in good shape. Sickness, disease and obesity cannot live within my spirit, mind or body.

I am fit! I am healthy! I am in great shape inside and out.

Whenever I hit a bump in the road or have a setback, **I always rise victoriously** over all challenges because I never give up or give in to negative circumstances. I reject all negative comments from others and choose to live my life, not someone else's. People may mean well, but **I am the captain of my ship** and God is my commander and chief who always leads me into perfect waters. When the storms of life come, I know that God will sustain me and keep me safe from all harm!

Chapter Five

Financial Life

Your finances and career are an area of life that few people have given much thought or planning. Some do not believe that they are entitled to living a successful and prosperous life. Many today believe that prosperity is either wrong or worldly? Prosperity has been misunderstood, misinterpreted and mishandled by many people. Is it wrong to have money? Is it our right? Are we all supposed to be rich? Is being poor more spiritual than being rich? These are all legitimate questions that we must come to grips with in order to effectively live a successful life.

I believe that poverty is a curse. What is poverty? Poverty is a state of being poor. A poor person is a person who goes without because he has no means to support himself and is supported by charity. God did not intend for us to be poor and living in poverty. In fact, we are to be in the position to help the poor and be financial blessings. Each of us has the ability to be good stewards of all that God has given to us financially and materially. We are to be good stewards of all that we have been given. It takes money to do good things and God does not desire for us to live like paupers. It is not spiritual to be a pauper. It is a curse.

If you are frustrated over money and finances then there is a problem. God did not intend for us to be broke and poor. God desires to bless us and pour out an abundance of wealth upon us all. This does not mean we will be millionaires but this does not mean we will be in the poor house either. I have seen people do great things with what God has given them. A little can go a long way if we honor God with our substance. It's not always what you don't have but what you do with what you do have. If you are spending money faster than you make it, then you have a problem. If you are in debt over your head then you have a problem. If you cannot or will not give then you have a problem. If you learn to manage money based on sound principles, it does not matter at which income level you are. A good steward will always manage his money and get along well.

One reason why you are not being blessed with more money may be because you have not learned to manage what you have correctly. God and the universe may not be able to trust you with more money. A good steward will be given more to manage when he proves that he is able to handle what he has. Another reason may be that you have doubted your ability to make money. Maybe you have told yourself the lie that being poor and broke is spiritual. It's actually a curse to be broke and unable to live life to its fullest. Living from paycheck to paycheck is a curse. Living in debt is a curse. Not being able to give is a curse. How can you be spiritual and a blessing to others when you have a broke mentality?

Have you settled for less than you are capable of achieving? Have you hidden your talents in a dead end job? Are you afraid to change and step out in faith to reach your full potential in God? Have you passed up opportunities that God has sent your way because you were scared, skeptical or negative? God does not want you to settle for less than you are able to achieve for Him. God wants you to live up to your full potential. God wants you to glorify Him by taking dominion and ruling the earth in your vocation or profession. This may require you to step out of your comfort zone and step out in faith. You may need to change some things in your life. You may need to work on your self-confidence.

You may need to learn how to dream and use your imagination. You may need to get more expertise and training. You may need to seek out help and advice. Whatever you need to do to live your life to its fullest extent –just do it!

Don't settle for a life of poverty and living a life of bondage. If there were no obstacles to get in the way, how would you like to live your life? What would you really like to do for God? What kind of aspirations would you have if money were no problem? What would be different in your life if you were not broke and living in poverty? If you could do anything in life, what would you be doing?

Maybe you need to start making some goals and reliving your childhood dreams. God gave you the ability to dream and imagine. He gave you a mind to think, reason and gain intellectual knowledge. He gave you creativity and the ability to make things appear from your imaginations. Everything we see in the world was first the thought of someone's imagination. What's going on in your mind? What kind of dreams do you have or have had? Are they good, wholesome desires that honor and glorify God? If so, pursue your dreams. Develop a plan to fulfill your destiny. You have a purpose and a destiny. You have talents and gifts. You were created to take dominion of your life. Get over your fears and go for it! Life is too short to live from paycheck to paycheck and live a life of poverty. Life can be exciting if we understand that we were created to master our lives and rule the earth.

Find a career you can excel in. I believe going into business for yourself could be the best thing that ever happened for you. A business you own can glorify God and advance His kingdom because you own and manage it for Him. When you desire to live up to your full potential, God and the universe will bless your efforts. This is and still remains the American dream. Working for somebody else may fulfill someone else's dreams but this probably will not fulfill yours. Jobs are ways to support our lives but many times they hold us back and put us in bondage. If you are happy at your job and are content with someone else controlling your life, then remain a servant to them, and do them a good job to the glory of God. However, if you feel you have more to accomplish, then begin now to look for ways to fulfill your destiny. Don't settle for less than reaching your full potential.

In your pursuit to fulfill your destiny you need to realize that you can fulfill your dreams! It is just as spiritual to be a businessman, doctor, lawyer, politician, electrician, scientist, entertainer, musician or artist as anything else in life that you do. Educate yourself and motivate yourself to take control over your career and finances. Write down your goals and dreams. Evaluate where you have been, where you want to go. Then make plans to change what needs to be changed. You can succeed and be financially prosperous. **IT** is your right!

There is within everyone a human urge for sound health, love, joy, peace, friendship, romance, and financial success! If you have lost that urge, **IT** is never too late to rekindle and renew the spirit of youth! There is within everyone the urge to live a wonderful life. The positive person thinks life is a grand opportunity to experience a high-energy life of sound health, love, joy, peace, hope, faith, and is motivated to take the necessary actions to make it so.

However, if **your negative self** has been in control of your life, then you are living in one or more of the following characteristics: mediocrity, poverty, criticism, ill health, loss of love, loss of freedom, greed, intolerance, revenge, bitterness, suspicion, jealousy, envy, lack, no self-control, argumentativeness, hatred, emulation, strife, discord, impatient, substance abuse, judgmental attitudes, sickness, obesity, disillusionment, defeat, arrogance, egotism, and all else that breeds the negative sort of self. Therefore, **we must affirm our positive self** and deny the negative self.

When the **negative self** is in charge, we perpetuate negativity within and without our life. We attract negativity into our "vibrational center" and become a breeding ground of fear and failure. But when your positive self is in control, it attracts into your vibrational center only those things that stimulate positive energy into your life. Some may call this the law of life and death while others call it the Law of Attraction. Life can be creative and fun; or it can be destructive and sad. It is a state of mind produced within. Mental attitude is a powerful energy that converts the brain into what we are thinking. This is the equivalent of an electro-magnet that acts like a magnet to attract the counterpart of one's dominating thoughts, good or bad.

All the tangible and intangible riches of life start with a **positive mental attitude**. Everything is a state of mind. The power of positive thinking is a prerequisite for positive living! Sound living requires sound thinking. The mind must think in terms of health and not in terms of illness to be healthy. This holds true for everything in life. If we fear anything, we become a magnet for the very thing we fear! There are seven basic fears which appear most in the minds of people which are the fear of poverty, criticism, ill health, loss of love, loss of freedom, old age and death. A positive mind always maintains the **hope** of achievement and the capacity for **faith**. Faith is an eternal elixir that produces positive expectation and hope. Faith is the basis for all so-called miracles and other mysteries that cannot be explained by logic or science. Faith is the power which transmutes the ordinary energies of thought into their reality. Faith mixed with prayer and meditation gives one immediate connection with the Infinite Intelligence of God that appropriates the Spiritual powers of the Cosmos. I like to call this Cosmic Power, the power and energy of God!

A positive mind produces a **willingness to share** one's blessings so that they may be multiplied and blessed. Life should be like a river that is never damned up. Riches are to be shared. When they are not, they lead to decay and death due to inaction and disuse. This is why life should be a labor of love! True love is the highest form of expression. It is always happily giving and blessing. A positive mind is an open mind that is **tolerant and respectful**. Having an open mind on all subjects at all times is a great challenge for negative people. An open mind opens the door to the greater riches of life. It also keeps us from being judgmental and critical in a negative sort of way.

A positive mind produces **self-disciplined people** who are the masters of their own fate. The person who is not the master of himself may never become the master of anything. Self-control and discipline are positive tools for success. Self-discipline not only leads to riches and great fortune, but it also leads to great humility and compassion for others. We are all fundamentally alike and have similar desires and emotions. Self-discipline helps us understand our emotions and our desires so that we can master them. All human activity is inspired by these basic desires and emotions: the emotion of love and sex, the desire for self-preservation and material gain, the emotion of anger and fear, the desire for freedom and self-expression, and the desire for spiritual meaning now and after death.

A positive mind produces a life that betters others. Our lives should be a blessing to others. If your life is not on track then this is a good indication that your mind is not being conditioned to accepting the riches of life. Just as the soil of a garden has to be prepared to produce a great crop, so must the mind of a person be prepared to create a productive life. **When one is ready for a thing, it is sure to appear!** Human progress has always been slow due to people being reluctant to accept new ideas. All the great minds of life have been ridiculed, scorned, and doubted. It is hard to believe that most everyone thought the world was flat, not round!

A positive mind is a **grateful mind** filled with gratitude! A positive person never takes anything for granted. Nothing is too big or too small to be grateful for. Material prosperity, sound physical health, peace of mind, the power of faith, hope, love, romance, wisdom, and all else are the result of a positive mind filled with gratitude for the blessings of such things. And as a result of being thankful, we immunize the mind against all negative mental attitudes that would like to creep in otherwise. Our most formidable adversary is our mind.

A positive mind is a mind with **definiteness of purpose**. A person without a definite purpose is a mind prone to fail and drift through life aimlessly. Drifters are subject to the thoughts and plans of others. Drifters typically allow others to think for them religiously, spiritually, politically, financially, morally and in every way. They depend on others to think for them and blindly trust others. A person without a definite purpose will drift through life and never experience true riches. Drifters usually settle for less than what life can offer them. While some may achieve a certain level of peace, they miss out on expanding and expressing their true God-given potential. All humans are born with the urge to be healthy, wealthy, happy and free, yet some succumb to the negative side of life.

This is why any **dominating desire**, plan, purpose, or attitude that is held in the mind consciously will eventually come to pass: good or bad. This is why drifters fulfill other people's desires by allowing their minds to be controlled by others. The subconscious mind acts on the thoughts it is given and carries out whatever it is programmed with. When a person develops self-reliance, personal initiative, enthusiasm, self-discipline and concentration of effort, mixed with faith and hope; success will soon follow! Success consciousness takes over as singleness of purpose takes over.

A positive mind will have the wisdom to **write out a complete, clear and definite statement** of definite purpose. This statement should describe precisely what you want, when you want it, how much you want, and what you will give in return for the realization of this definite purpose. Make your plan flexible enough to permit changes at any time you are inspired to do so! God and the universe may present to you a far superior plan than any you create. Be open and receptive to God and the Universe!

Positive minds will surround themselves with **positive people** who are in agreement with their definite purpose. Hanging out with negative people will only pull you down. If someone is not where you want to be in life, then you may want to reject their advice. People mean well, but people are for the most part, drifters who have no clue. However, if you find people who are like-minded and agree with your definite purpose, you can form a master alliance of minds to assist each other in the attainment of your desires. A positive mind will follow a **Success Formula!**

1. **Have a written and specific mission statement** that describes in detail what your definite purpose in life is. Have a written plan that specifies how much money you want to make, how you will make it, and what you are willing to do and give up to make it. Create a dream board, dream book or visual pictures of what you want that you can look at every day in different

places. If you have not done this, now is the time to develop them! And remember, a jack of all trades is a master of none. Sell out to one mission.

2. **Don't let anyone steal your dream**! People mean well but they will hold you back. If you want to move forward, you will have to burn bridges and take advice from people who can assist you to move forward. Don't let others steal your joy or desire to get ahead and fulfill your dreams! There are dream makers, dream takers, and dream fakers! Decide that you will succeed no matter what other people say or do! To move up sometimes we have to move on from mediocre people and well-meaning people in our lives. **If you don't control your life somebody else will! Develop supreme confidence in yourself and your own abilities!**

3. **Develop a burning desire**! Catch on fire and the world will watch you burn! Enthusiasm is contagious! If you know who you are and where you are going, people will take notice! Read, listen, and educate yourself on how to be a magnetic leader! Learn proper people skills and be willing to CHANGE! Be willing to take constructive criticism, and then be willing to take your medicine and change for the better. Things do not change, we do! Everyone can create a new self! To grow we must change! It is passion that causes people to stay up late and get up early. Take personal responsibility for your life and refuse to accept anything but success.

4. **Develop a dogged determination** to follow through and never give up. Period! Follow through with your dreams even in the midst of criticism, negative circumstances, obstacles, and negative people! You can if you think you can. What you believe, you can achieve! Direct your thoughts, control your emotions, and ordain your destiny! Never give up! Big shots were little shots that kept on shooting!

5. **Speak and affirm your dreams, visions, and goals!** What we can imagine, what we say, what we confess, what we declare, what

we think on and have supreme faith in will come to pass! What we think, what we envision, and what we say affects who we are and what we become! The tongue speaks and the body listens! Don't be hung by the tongue! Say what you want, speak what you want and never waiver! All negative talk is destructive and will always hold you back.

6. **Be a crusader!** Great opportunities are attacked! It is not luck or anything else that determines success. Stop making excuses to justify failure and determine to be a winner! Construct your determination with sustained effort, controlled attention, and concentrated energy! Catch of fire and the world will come to watch you burn!

Chapter Six

Social Life

Man was not created to be an island unto himself. God created us as social beings that need time to enjoy people and activities. God did not place us here to be alone and bored. God wants us to have a good time and enjoy life. There is nothing wrong with having good, clean fun. A dull life makes a dull person. An active social life is healthy and helps us to be better people. Your social life will begin with your family and extend out to friends at work, church and other places. Your social life is important. We all need to have a balanced life of social activity and recreation.

People need people. While some are more social than others, we all need to take time for activities that stimulate fun and conversation. We all need to learn proper social manners and graces. The fellowship and fun helps us to balance out the other pressures of life and allows us to unwind and relax. This is why we need a balance of active and relaxing activities to allow ourselves to rejuvenate. In our fast-paced lives we need to find time for some rest and relaxation with family and friends. It is healthy and will enhance your life. In fact, hobbies, sports and participation in the arts have been proven to improve your mind and body. It is never too late to start. You are only as old as you think you are! Maybe there is something you have desired to do all your life but are afraid to give it a try. Let me encourage you to step out and do it. You have nothing to lose and a lot to gain.

Discover ways to become more active and creative when trying to have fun, unwind and relax. Talk with your spouse. Start a new hobby. Get involved with activities that place you around positive people who like to have fun and laugh. Laughter is good for you. It is healing and uplifting. He who has a merry heart has a fruitful life. A cheerful heart produces a smile but sorrow breaks our will to succeed. A happy person with a cheerful heart is a medicine that cures disease, but a broken spirit contributes to poor health. Learn to love people and learn to make friends. Be proactive. Don't settle for the easy chair or become a couch potato. Video games and television do not help in this area of your life. In fact, I believe the television set is responsible for more negativity in life than all other things combined. Enjoy life and enjoy people. You will become a happier person and you will feel better. Just remember that social activities are not everything and you should not be consumed with being entertained all the time. Enjoy watching TV and playing games, but do so in moderation!

One of the pitfalls of religion is the preaching and teaching of legalistic religious leaders that condemn having fun! I mention this because so many religious people are unhappy and have been convinced that dancing, a social drink, or going to moves, etc. is worldly and sinful. I believe as long as we are having fun and are not harming or violating anyone, and then go for it! Religion will have you bound up in rules and regulations and have you uptight, judgmental, and miserable. So set yourself free from religious, fundamentalist legalism! Live life and have some fun! Live and love life with all your heart and soul and enjoy all that life has to offer. I would like to encourage you and empower you to enjoy life and have some recreational fun! All work and no play will indeed make life dull. So rediscover the curiosity of life and go enjoy all of God's creation. Life was meant to be enjoyed so by all means go out and have

This is IT!

some fun! Balance out your life with equal amounts of fun and work so that you can be better at everything you do.

As I conclude this chapter, I would like to illustrate how we need friends and comradery in the journey of life. We are in this life together and sometimes we find people along the way to help us complete our journey. In the movie, 'The Wizard of Oz', we see how Dorothy and her new found friends follow the **Yellow Brick Road to success!**

Many people remember watching Dorothy struggling to find her way home in this famous movie. After being trapped in a tornado storm in Kansas, Dorothy awakes to find herself in a strange place away from home. Dorothy is like many people who sometimes find themselves struggling with life and wondering what life is all about. That is why I believe this story can help us all realize life is an adventure and has its ups and downs. In the movie, the tornado represented the turmoil she felt in her life and the confusion that comes with living. Many times in our struggle with life we have to discover the true meaning of life through adversity and a discovery process that requires walking down the "yellow brick road" of life!

We are all on a unique journey of discovery and adventure that we call the experiences of life. Life is all about discovering who you are and learning the real truth about life. **The Wizard of Oz** is a great story of how we all can arrive home safely and discover true peace and happiness in life. Most people live in a "black and white" world that represents who they are and where they are in life. Some people settle for this "black and white" life but some wake up and begin to ask how they can travel life "in color" and begin to walk down the "streets of gold", the "yellow brick road" of discovery.

Frustration, defeat, confusion, and the struggles of life can be our friends if we let them drive us to ask new questions and question life on its present level. **When you have the "guts"** to ask the questions about what life is really about, who we are, and how we can go from a "black and white" to a "colorful" life, you begin the journey to self-discovery! Life is meant to be an eternal journey of self-discovery and expanding awareness to the knowledge of more of what is possible for YOU! As you begin to discover who you are and your awareness grows, your thoughts and beliefs will change. Change is difficult and requires questioning yourself, your parents, your teachers, your friends, your religious and political leaders and all the systems of the world!

New possibilities will emerge as you ask the tough questions and open yourself to learning more about yourself and this wonderful world and universe we live in! True change begins and ends with a change in YOU! This is what happened to Dorothy and she found her way home. YOU can also find your way home! You can find true peace and happiness apart from the "black and white" life that engulfs the majority of people today who are more inclined to follow the "status quos" of the world. I believe that if YOU are still reading this, YOU are not willing to settle for the status quos of the world. You are looking to expand and grow in knowledge to the truth that will set you free!

So I hope you, like Dorothy, and many others, will begin to awaken to new possibilities! If you have grown tired of all the negative energy of life and desire to experience life the way it was meant to be, then you are ready to move forward and experience a new life of love, joy, peace, goodness and beauty! As Dorothy found a person she could trust to guide her home, you can trust yourself to discover a pathway to true peace and happiness. YOU are ready to follow the "Yellow Bick Road" of LIFE!

Now we will discover how each of the characters in the story represents a specific truth in finding our way home. Life is a journey to discover more about who we are and the type of life we are all capable of creating. At some point, we all have asked the typical questions of life and have sought guidance and help along the way. The danger is surrendering our mind and destiny to the experiences and conclusions of others. It is good to inquire and ask, but whenever we surrender our lives and wills to political, scientific, religious or social philosophies, we stop the expansion and growth of our individual life.

In Dorothy's journey down the yellow brick road, **Glinda the Good Witch of the North** represents the need to follow the trusted guide of wisdom. North always points up. Wisdom by definition is the logical conclusion of truth. Truthful wisdom sets us free when it is applied in a sensible and reasonable way. Wisdom is being able to understand truth and apply it in such a way that it benefits everyone in every way. Wisdom is learning that truth is loving, compassionate, peaceful, joyful, and all encompassing. Wisdom is the ability to judge anything we learn about with this all encompassing philosophy. This is why we have to be careful not to fall into a system of beliefs that contradicts the spirit of wisdom that comes with truth.

The Wicked Witch of the West represents the obstacles of life that attempt to stop us from moving forward in our journey of life. People mean well but people will hold you back! Most people fail to move forward because they have a **fear** of what others might think if they move away from their systems of belief. The belief systems we have grown up with, adopted, or joined need to be challenged many times. This kind of change is always the hardest. Peer pressure and the fear of being considered a fool are powerful weapons that prevent us from growing and expanding.

Along the way, Dorothy picks up **three companions** who accompany her on her journey. These three companions represent three critical qualities that we all need to live life to its fullest extent. The **Scarecrow** represents the need for us to think, imagine, dream, create, reason, contemplate, challenge, and be intuitive. In each and every person is the power to understand life and live life according to our individuality. We are capable and have the ability to co-create, expand, and grow on every level! People who cannot tap into this resource are bound to be as the Scarecrow who lived life in fear and at the mercy of others.

The Tin Man represents the need for us to be loving, compassionate, sympathetic, empathetic, merciful, caring, understanding, longsuffering, and forgiving. This love needs to be directed inward and outward! If what you believe causes you hate or dislike anyone, it is wrong! Love is patient and is kind. It never keeps score and is never proud! Love covers a multitude of failure! Life is about discovering the truth and heart of love. Once you have discovered true love you will be set free!

The Lion represents the need to have faith and the power of belief. We all need the courage to face life head on and face all the fears, challenges and obstacles that may try to stop us! It takes guts to live sometimes!

Courage comes from within and we must brave the storms and boldly go where few travel! I call this intestinal fortitude! As we develop the belief that we are here to expand, grow, and create a magnificent life of beauty, we can then, by faith, be brave enough to be who we are.

As we continue down the Yellow Brick Road, Dorothy and her new friends set off to see the great Wizard who they believe will help them with their needs. When they arrive, the Wizard demands they bring the broomstick of the Wicked Witch of the West back to him before he grants them the help they seek. Dorothy and her friends are now forced to face their greatest fears to receive the help they hoped to gain from the Wizard. Their desire to receive what they want is greater than their fear of the Wicked Witch. In their struggle with the Witch, the answer to her demise occurs while they are fighting the powers of the Witch. All it takes is a bucket of water to dissolve the Witch and she slowly melts away. Likewise, the struggles of life often bring us the answers we are looking for. If you are in the battle, you have a chance to win. If you retreat, run, or give up, you can never win. Many of life's struggles are won when we least expect it and in unexpected ways. This is why we must never give up! We must face our fears with courage, faith and hope.

Dorothy and her new friends start their journey back to the Wizard with the broomstick, and with a new found enthusiasm and expectation that their needs will now be meet. As they enter the Wizard's palace, Toto the dog unveils a simple old man who had been behind the fearful Wizard all along. The illusion of a Wizard who will rescue them is unmasked! So many times in life we are looking to the Wizards of the world like politicians, preachers, teachers, gurus, parents, friends, leaders, and the like for answers. The simple old man tells them that the answer to their needs is not to be found in him or a Wizard. The answers are always found within them. So he encourages them by symbolically awarding them superficial acknowledgments of what they all inwardly possess.

The Wizard offers Dorothy a ride home as the story goes, and then accidently and providentially ends up leaving her behind. Devastated, Dorothy now turns to the good witch Glinda who had been guiding her along the Yellow Brick Road. Through the help of her guide she realizes that the answer was "within" her the whole time! The Scarecrow annoyingly asked the good witch Glinda why she did not tell her before? Glinda responds by saying that she would not have believed me because she had to learn IT for herself!

Dorothy is now ready to go home! How? By accepting and being thankful for everything she has right now. As she embraces this most powerful thought, she embraces the truth, and her journey home begins. When she arrives home, she is filled with love, peace and joy! Life is the pursuit of love, peace, joy, and hope that is found within. It is never found in the systems or Wizards of the world. Dorothy is now ready to live! She has found peace. She embraces her life and God and the universe grant her desires! She stops struggling and starts living! She overcomes her fears and takes control of her life. No longer does she allow the witches and wizards of the world to control, manipulate, dominate or pull her down. Dorothy and her friends find what they need together in the journey of life! We are all in this journey together. We all need each other in the process of finding the truth that will set us all free!

It is agreed upon by all that the law of sowing and reaping delivers whatever we choose to create, good or bad! You are a summary of your belief systems and your life is a reflection of those beliefs. The good news is that you can create a new you by the choices you make today. When you decide to take full responsibility for your life, you can create a new and better life. God and the universe only desire to love you and allow you to expand and mature into a life filled with all beauty! The journey of life is indeed a Yellow Brick Road that will respond to your inner most thoughts and desires! The choice is yours. I am not who I was or who I will be. I am who I choose to be NOW! So be IT! I AM that I AM!

Chapter Seven

The Science of Life

THE SCIENCE OF LIFE IS the art and science of living a life of beauty, happiness, love, peace and vibrant health in every area of our life. **Life Science** seeks to develop all sides of our life, nature, and being, whereby, we live in harmony within as we live in union with God and the Universe. The universe includes not only ourselves, people, nature, and our environment, but also the cosmic energy of God that interconnects us within and without.

Life Science teaches us that **We are Spirit** and our essence is made up of light and energy that energizes all of creation. We contain the life-force of the universe! God expresses himself throughout all of the cosmos and gives life to all. The essence of our life is energy that comes from the energy of the universe. This energy activates the biological life and mental life of mankind and all intelligence. We are a network of energy and intelligence that is in a constant state of communication within and without, spiritually, physically, emotionally, mentally and universally with the entire cosmos. **We are cosmic beings!**

Therefore, we are a dynamic bundle of energy that encompasses many expressions of God in our spirit, mind, and body. **We have the potential to reflect the image of God's** nature in our personality, character, aspirations and dreams, imagination, creativity, intellect, productivity, morality, and in any other way we live. Therefore, as we attune with our true self and the Cosmos, we can live up to our full potential in every aspect of life! We were created to take dominion, rule, reign and live a life of abundance. It is in our essence. It is our potential.

The Science of Life recognizes that we are designed by God to live on earth in a physical body that houses our spirit and makes us a living soul. We are spiritual beings in a physical body experiencing Earth and the entire Cosmos. This is why in the study of Quantum Physics so many scientists are coming to acknowledge that there has to be a God or Infinite Intelligence that permeates the universe and the cosmos. Science is our friend and **God is the great scientific architect of the universe who desires for you to reach your full potential in life!**

Therefore, if we desire to live a life of beauty, love, joy, goodness, peace and tranquility, we must desire to know ourselves spiritually, physically, mentally and emotionally. This is why you need to **challenge yourself to expand your awareness**. Open yourself up to know yourself! Be open and observing but don't be gullible! Embrace your spiritual self. Replace life damaging choices with life affirming choices. Whenever we choose to make a change in any way, we ultimately affect more change to come.

The Science of Life includes the study of biology, physiology, psychology, philosophy, anthropology, chemistry, mathematics, etymology, spirituality, theology and all else that is at our disposal. However, this does not mean we become gullible and take everything at face value. Truth is truth but sometimes so called facts are just educated guesses which are highly speculative and shaded to prove one's position in a logical and reasonable way that may be right but may also be wrong! I believe that all areas of life can harmonize, including religion and science as long as we don't have an agenda to begin with. So wipe the slate clean but be cautious and always scrutinize everything.

Key one to living an optimal life is the **acknowledgment of Infinite Intelligence**. This may sound elementary but even people who claim to know God really don't know God at all. They may have mentally assented to God but have never really experienced the **Infinite Intelligence** which is the spirit of revelation and wisdom and knowledge of ourselves within and without. Also, I believe that many who claim to reject God or the belief in God are really just rejecting religion. When someone truly understands who God is, they will acknowledge that there is Infinite Intelligence that is behind all there is. The universe in all its wonder and complexity is not the result of an accident or happenstance. This wonderful world and universe we live in demands the belief in a Creator and a designer.

I believe that **all of creation declares the existence of Infinite Intelligence.** What mankind has discovered in the sciences, proves the existence of Infinite Intelligence that shows up in every aspect of life. The existence of Infinite Intelligence can be proven in science but most Infinite Intelligence exists in the heart and soul of mankind. We are made in God's image. God is Spirit and we are spirit. God is not a gray haired man with a beard and lightning bolts in his hands. God is not some figure we have created in our minds or in religion. Your reference points of seeing and experiencing God is and has been shaped by how you see Him based on personal beliefs and interpretations of what you hold to be true. Beliefs create your reality. **This is why we have so many churches and different religions**. It is uncomfortable to acknowledge that you may be wrong about God and religion. It is hard to change strong belief systems that have been engrained into the fabric of your life. But if you want to expand and grow, you may have to change your belief systems.

So what does it mean to be born-again? **Regeneration** is the process of re-setting your reference points and changing the way you think and act on many levels, including religious beliefs. To be **born-again** is more than just saying a prayer. To be born-again is the beginning of a process whereby you become spiritually aware and begin to discover yourself rather than a religious system! It is God's desire for you to know yourself and for you to experience **love** in every area of your life. Being born-again is a process whereby we attune to ourselves spiritually, mentally, and emotionally. It is a place where we become **self-conscious** rather than **flesh-conscious**! When we are attuned within we experience a state of being in which we start living in harmonious reaction with God and the universe. God's character and desires become our character and desires. In this state, you spontaneously bloom and produce godly intention, insight, imagination, creativity, peace, intellect and all fruits of the Spirit such as love, joy, peace, etc. You have union with God!

Who you are is more important than what you do or claim to know about external truth. Being born-again is not about keeping religious rules, it is about becoming a **Christ-Conscious** person who reflects the image God in all you do and say. What it is not about is waiting for a future event where God waves a magic wand over us and we become like Christ. Being born-again is a process whereby the fabric of God is woven into our lives in every aspect of our existence. It is 'not' about trying to be like him by living by a religious code. Union with God is about knowing who you are without all the pressure or stress of being someone you are not! God loves you no matter what, and He is patient with you wherever you are in your walk with Him. We are in a process and sometimes we become frustrated when we fail to see this. **God is the most misrepresented person** in today's world of religion and non-religious systems of mankind.

Infinite Intelligence (God) is many things in the full scope of the world, but God is first and foremost **love!** God is not out to 'get you' in a bad way, God is out to 'get you' like a lover who just meet you and longs to spend every moment together. God proved this love to us by allowing the failures of man to crucify Christ. God loves you! He cares for you! God wants His very best for you! Learn to love yourself in a godly way. Learn to accept this love unconditionally and realize God wants you to experience an abundant life of love, joy, and peace! When you understand that God is love, you can love yourself and love others the way God loves you. You no longer see the failures of yourself and others, you only see the potential!

Beware! In seeking to know God, realize that the goal of experiencing God is to know ourselves! It is not so that we can be on a mountain top all the time singing, dancing, and going from one emotional experience to another. The goal is not to find the perfect place to serve or have a ministry where you can fulfill yourself. We have to know ourselves and then serve! The goal is not to be a theologian either. It is good to study but the Scriptures should direct us to look within and not at a book! Intellectualism and knowledge can be good if balanced with the Spirit.

The **second key to living an optimal life is trusting in Your True Self.** Trusting in Self is essential and required if we desire to continue the process of living an abundant life. It is one thing to have intellectual knowledge and another to know your true self. There is this 'other self' within us that we have to discover! With all the noise of the world, it is hard to find this person. The mind can wander and the soul can vacillate, but our true essence is eternal and constant. Your true self will never allow fear, discouragement and the like to be in control. If you are discouraged or defeated in any way then you have allowed your mind and soul to rule your life! People who drift through life and allow others to control them are not attuned to their true self. When we look within and learn to know our self, we are living the abundant life. We are in control of our destiny. We are alive!

If things are tough, then maybe there needs to be some change in your life? Maybe you just need to learn patience. Maybe you are reaping what you have sown? Sometimes we have to go through hell to get to heaven. That makes heaven even sweeter! Once we know what death tastes like, we know a good thing when we get it! Experiencing the opposite of our true self helps us truly understand and appreciate the goodness of God and the cosmos.

The third key to living an optimal life is reprogramming the mind. The mind is one of greatest battlefields of all time. The mind can be ever-changing and struggling with what is truth. This can set the stage for competition within and without, with self and with others. Most people desire absolute truth that can direct their lives through many avenues such as religion, politics, philosophy, education, etc. Who do we submit to? Who is right and who is wrong? Where do we find the truth? Which religious view is correct and which is wrong? And on and on we go.

God gave us a brain with the capacity to think, imagine, reason, and solve. We possess intellect and wisdom. We have the ability to create and invent. **Our minds are powerful computers** that can be programmed and re-programmed to perform on different levels. In the regenerative process we have to be transformed by the renewing of our minds. This is why we need to be careful what we read, watch and feed our brains. Be selective in whom you allow to influence you. You can learn from everyone but not everyone has all the truth. Sometimes we can learn from people what to do and what not to do! **I always say, 'If someone is not where you want to be in life, then you probably should not take their advice on many things!'** The mind of a person is the most powerful computer ever invented. It was designed to sustain all biological functions of the body through the subconscious mind so that we don't have to think about those functions! The source of all direction and coordination of bodily functions, thoughts, facts, and knowledge are stored there and operate automatically based on God-given programming in the subconscious.

The subconscious mind is connected to Infinite Intelligence and is communicating constantly with the universe! The mind is telepathic and has the capacity to sense and pick up things in the spiritual and physical dimensions of the cosmos. This is why all of us have sensed things and felt things in our spirit that have warned us, helped us, and urged us to pray for someone or call someone. It is more than just a premonition. It is what I believe is the sixth sense of man that has been lost.

I believe that as man has become more connected to the physical aspects of life and its fleshly desires and feelings, he has become less spiritually connected and oriented to the higher vibrations of the universe. I would call this **the higher-conscious** that has been neglected due to mankind being more attuned to the physical and material life. The good news is that we can, through prayer, meditation and intent of thought, connect to this higher-consciousness and begin to tune in to the spiritual domain of the universe.

This brings us to the conscious mind. The conscious mind has the power to direct thoughts, reason, exercise will-power, make life changing choices, make decisions and re-shape the sub-conscious by reprogramming it with new ideas and thoughts. Change can be directed through the control of thought habits! You are what you are because of what you think about what you say, what you read, and what you feed the brain with on a daily basis. God has given us the power of choice and the right to control our minds, thoughts, and habits. We are all a bundle of habits. Self-discipline is the only means by which one's habits can be controlled and directed. The potential to change and reach new levels of life is beyond comprehension! Through faith, will-power, and Infinite Intelligence, we have the power to change and control the nature of our thoughts. In doing so, we can change for the better!

Remember, we can open our minds to the wrong things. We don't need to feed our minds with junk and we don't need to hear more sermons on how bad we are. We need more sermons and more help with recognizing the ability we have to change with the tools God has given us. We can reprogram our minds to live an optimal life of health and vitality. The mind can be transformed and renewed! It requires us to cast out the bad programming of our lives up to now, stop listening to the broadcasting stations of negativity, and then tune into God's broadcasting system of faith, hope and love!

So we must realize that whatever we put into our mind is our responsibility! We are where we are due to what we have been programmed to believe. Whatever you have allowed to be put into your brain has affected your thought, attitudes, feelings, actions and the results you are experiencing in life now. Whatever you listen to, whatever you read, whoever you associate with, whatever you dream about and think about makes you who you are and positions you where you are in life.

If you want to change your life, then change what you put into your mind in all these ways. Maybe it's time to change what you listen to, who you hang out with, what you read, and what you believe! Start today to retrain and reprogram your mind. As you change these things you can take control of your life. **As a man thinks, so he is!** Don't allow anyone to rob you of your God-given right to live an abundant life of love, joy, peace and all that is good and wholesome. Program your mind to improve yourself and you will begin to experience a more abundant life! **Cast out the stinking thinking thoughts of the past and begin now to imagine and believe in the new you!**

As I conclude this chapter, I would like to share a **Declaration of Religious Science Principles** that I believe is truth and will set us free! I believe these principles can unite us rather than divide us in our journey of life. I believe we will enter a new age of science, religion, politics, and philosophy of life that will promote unity in the world and ultimately bring world peace!

We believe in God, the Almighty Living Spirit who is Indestructible, absolute and the First Cause of all the Cosmos. God manifests in and through all, but is not absorbed by all. The cosmos is the body of God that reflects God intellectually, emotionally, creatively, and logically in a myriad of ways. God is Infinite Intelligence, Universal Spirit, and Material Reality. The material world represents God's intentions and extensions of Divinity.

We believe that God is the absolute being of pure oneness and unity; the source of all power and stability. God is the creative force of all the cosmos and a flow of loving energy that flows in and through the interior of this oneness. The Breathe of God or Universal Spirit carries the forces (energies) of God into the cosmos and is eternally echoing the energies of God. Furthermore, we believe that God in character is both male and female.

We believe in the Unity of all life and that God is in all and sustains all by the power of Infinite Intelligence and Universal Spirit. Infinite Intelligence represents all the Divine Laws of the Universe that are absolute and eternally immutable. Universal Spirit is the light and energy of God that produces Creation and sustains the cosmos. The material world is a reflection of God's infinite intelligence, imagination, and creativity. God is the power behind all things that exist.

We believe that all humans are incarnations of God. Humans are the crown of glory of all creation and have been endued with the responsibility to rule, reign, and expand the presence and reality of God. In this esteemed position we have great responsibility and accountability to expand the true nature of God in every aspect of life. We are not God. We are extended images of God, and in essence, one with God. God is self-existent and we are co-creators with God to expand the image of God through-out the entire cosmos.

We believe that as humans we can commune with God personally and receive revelation and inspiration through divine communication. As we attune with God we are able to receive direct revelation from God and be guided into all Truth. We are all surrounded by Infinite Intelligence and Universal Spirit that is forever expanding and providing continuity and immortality to us all.

We believe the Kingdom of God is within man and that to know God is to know our self. God is not found in a religious building or a religious book. We have to look inward to experience who we are and who God is. This is why we believe that prayer and meditation are essential and necessary to enter into true bliss.

We believe that God is Love. We believe He is merciful and forgiving. The fall of mankind mentioned in sacred scripture revolves around the belief that we live in a dual world of good and evil. The tree of the knowledge of good and evil was not a real tree but the ability of humans to choose a life of duality. Duality causes confusion, divisiveness, discord, distress, and the misuse of energy from a human perspective. Energy will be expressed either positively if we are attuned within and with God, or negatively, if we are attuned to just our self and our environmental influences.

The Divine energy within us must find an outlet. Humans can suppress this energy and then experience a 'blow-up' just as a pipe will only withstand so much pressure before it bursts! This is why we should find something that we love to do that will allow us to express our self and loose the energies of life into action and transmute this power in a positive, creative way. Otherwise, we will fall prey to our own devices and create calamity in and around us. That is why sacred scriptures teach that to eat from the knowledge of good and evil ends up destroying us. A double-minded man is unstable in all his ways! But once we attune to God within we realize our own divinity. We realize that our true self is a divine being on a divine journey. We realize that we are sent here as spiritual entities to grow and expand the cosmos. Once this is realized we can escape the prison of duality.

We believe in the Law of Love. God is Love and we are Love! Love conquers all and love casts out all fear and negativity. If we do all in the power and divinity of true love, we can do no wrong! God created us to live, laugh and love! The law of love emancipates our duality and empowers us to do all in the spirit and revelation of love!

We believe that God is Spirit and that we should worship God in Spirit and in Truth. Worship is about connecting to God and the Cosmos in the spiritual dimensions. While music and other forms of external stimuli can assist us to worship God, worship is ultimately connecting inwardly and then outwardly with God and the universe.

We believe that Jesus Christ was an Anointed Son of God who provided a pattern and a way to enter into Truth. Jesus the Anointed one always pointed people to God the Father, and never himself. We believe that a relationship should be developed with the Oneness of God and not a singular person. Jesus taught that what he did, we could even greater! Jesus located the Kingdom of God within himself and pointed the way to Eternal Reality. Jesus was embodied with the divinity which comes through the anointing of the Universal Spirit and Mind of God. That is why we must as also become anointed or 'Christ-Conscious'. As we call upon Jesus we are in reality calling upon his pattern and his ways. To confess Christ is to affirm the Universal Spirit and Infinite Intelligence within us. Affirming the divinity of Jesus who was a living embodiment of the Christ-Consciousness allows us to affirm our own divinity and Christ-Consciousness. As the human gives way to the Divine, Christ is revealed in you! This is the mystery of all the ages revealed in all Truth! It is **Christ in YOU, the hope of glory!**

We believe that God has ordained that there be a gathering of those who are 'Christ conscious' to promotes the unity of God in all the cosmos and encourages people to mature, grow, and be empowered to live a Christ-Conscious life. We believe that we are all one with God and that the purpose of these gatherings is for the Spiritual Director to empower people to know who they are in God and discover their own Divinity.

We believe that God is personal to all who will discover this indwelling divine presence. The ultimate goal for us all is to discover our own true divinity and to be released from discord, disease, disillusionment, division, and double-mindedness. Through the power of this enlightenment, we believe that we can control our minds, control our bodies, and control our lives to the glory of God! We believe this to be true and available to all who desire to be saved and enlightened.

Chapter Eight

What the Hell?

Is God mad as hell? This study could turn out to be a heated topic! Hell is something we have all thought about and have personal opinions about. We like to tell people to 'go to hell' and we like to threaten people with going to hell! So, what is Hell? Where is it? Is Hell a literal place? Is hell a fairy tale? Is it simply a troubled mental state here on Earth? Is Hell a literal barbeque pit of flame and smoke? Will the wicked burn forever and forever and forever? Will the wicked eventually be annihilated? Will everyone eventually be saved from Hell? Do people have worms eating on them? What will happen to those billions of people who never heard the Gospel? Will there be a second chance? Is God mad as hell? Does God take pleasure in torturing and punishing people with no mercy? What about backsliders or those who commit suicide? Is there a purgatory? These are just some of the questions people ask about hell. So, what the hell does the bible say about hell?

First of all, the modern conceptions of heaven and hell have their origins in the ancient Egyptian culture where Moses lived, and from worldwide philosophers of all cultures who influenced the thoughts of Christians. The most influential writer about hell was a man named Dante Alighieri. He who wrote a poem called, La Divina Commedia, written in three parts: Hell, Purgatory, and Paradise. It was a comedy written to ridicule religious concepts during his day. This basis was from concepts of the philosophers Plato and Virgil. Plato influenced Greek thought and Virgil influenced Roman thought and many of the beliefs of the Roman Catholic Church. This poem was a lurid account of a dismal hell which caught the attention of the world in Dante's day and on into the modern day. The Catholic theologian, Augustine, popularized the view of purgatory and purgatorial fire that would be a place of purifying those who needed further cleansing of the soul before going to heaven.

Church politics have used hell to control, manipulate, dominate and influence the masses to believe in their systems of religion or else suffer in the fires of Hell! It has been used as a tool to condemn people and threaten them into submitting to church doctrines so the church could gain control over people's lives. Come to my tent and support my cause or you will go to hell! Sound familiar?

Second, the word hell does not appear in the original languages of the bible. In the King James Bible and in most modern bibles, the old English word 'hellel' or hell was a word that meant a hole in the ground that was covered up. It was a dark and silent place-a grave for something or someone! For instance, people in ancient times would put their potatoes in hell for the winter. Unfortunately the King James Bible and most modern translations continued with this misapplied translation and have obscured five words and phrases that are translated 'hell' in the bible. This alone should be a clue as to why there is confusion and disagreement over what hell is or is not!

So, what does the bible really say about hell? To begin our study of the word Hell we will uncover the meanings of the five words or phrases translated as hell in the bible. In studying these words, we will begin to uncover the true meaning of hell and understand what the bible really says. The first word translated hell is the Hebrew word **Sheol** that depicted the place of death when a person died, the grave. It is where the body rested and was turned back into the dust of the earth. Some schools of theology saw this as a resting place of sleep and some saw Sheol as a place where the spirits of people resided until summoned by God. The Jewish religion did not teach that we go to heaven or hell when we die. Most believed it was a sleeping state of a person until God resurrected them from the realm of the dead. **Judaism** did not have a definitive or specific doctrine about the afterlife.

Judaism also believed there was a **Book of Life** or **The Book of Remembrance** where the forgiven and faithful were recorded. However, some mystics and orthodox traditions taught about a purgatory or waiting room where the shortcomings and negative actions of sinners could be purged. Then they could be transferred into **The Book of Life** before entering into the ages to come, i.e. (Eternity). Most Hebrew traditions believed in a world to come where the soul is reborn. The wicked were annihilated in the fire of God's judgment and became ashes after 11 months of punishment (from one Sabbath Moon to another). Those who were corrected and purified entered eternity and the wicked ceased to be. In the **Rosh-Hashanah** celebration of the Jewish New Year, a prayer is sometimes prayed so that one can be sealed in the Book of Life. In the Liturgy it is prayed: "May we and all your people, The House of Israel, be remembered and inscribed in the Book of Life". Blessing, peace and prosperity were prayed for that they would have a life of peace and goodness.

The second word translated hell is the Greek word **Hades** used in mythological writings to depict the underworld where the dead were ruled by the god, Hades. Homer and Philo used this term in their writings to describe the unseen, invisible world of dead people. All kinds of mythical stories abound about Hades and what goes on in the realms of the dead. Many modern movies and TV programs use these imaginary stories to perpetuate the belief in an afterlife in some fashion or another. All cultures from the beginning of time have told stories about the afterlife. All religions have taught some form of afterlife whether it is literal or spiritual in some way. The original languages of Jesus were translated into Greek and Hades was used just like hell is used today to depict the place of the dead.

The writers of the New Testament used pagan, apocalyptic and contemporary terms of their day to communicate spiritual realities and truth in their writings, much like we speak today in contemporary terms that we understand. However, in doing so, many mythological beliefs have mistakenly been used to understand the realities of afterlife. Why? Because we fail to study the original intent of the writers and God! **Hades** is a word that the Hebrew-Jewish people used in place of the word **Sheol** in Greek speaking countries. In fact, the **LXX** Septuagint, which was the Old Testament Bible translated into Greek, was the most popular Bible the writers of the New Testament used to study and preach from. It was never meant to support the beliefs of pagan mythology. The study of words and their meanings have been lost in modern day Christianity. This has encouraged the rebirth of pagan beliefs in the church today. If you only study the King James Bible or a modern translation without studying the original languages, etymology, etc., you will mistakenly misinterpret the Bible with your cultural mindset rather than mindsets of those who wrote the Bible.

The third word translated hell in the Bible is the Greek word **Tartaros.** This Greek word is used once in **2 Peter 2:4** where it refers to the noun, found in the First book of **Enoch,** as the place of incarceration of 200 fallen angels guarded by the archangel Uriel. It mentions nothing about human souls being sent there after life. In Greek mythology Tartaros was a place of punishment for the dead. Homer called it a black hole with iron bar gates and bronze walls far below Hades. This was where the evil ones went who committed heinous crimes. This word was translated erroneously in the King James Bible and many modern translations as well with the word **Hell.**

The fourth word translated hell is the Greek word **Gehenna:** This is the word for a valley on the south west side of Jerusalem on the border between Judah and Benjamin called Ben-hinnom. It was here where King Ahab, Josiah, and Manasseh defiled the place by allowing idolatrous practices such as worshipping false gods, and burning their children on alters to Moloch. Jeremiah prophesied a great slaughter there of the citizens of Jerusalem due to forsaking their God and serving other gods.

Jewish apocalyptical writers called this place the entrance to **Sheol.** It was considered an intermediate state of the godless dead during the rebellion right before the flood that Noah experienced. During Jesus' day it had turned into a garbage dump to dispose of rubbish, dead carcasses of animals and diseased people. It burned constantly and smelled with the stitch of death and rottenness. It was a horrific place with holocaustic imagery. One can see why this place was defiled. It was a perfect image to depict the evil doings of mankind. It was an imagery that Jesus used to warn people what was in store for all who forsook God and lived rebellious lives of evil. Jesus used this analogy to parallel the future judgments of God where the just and unjust would inherit what they had sown while living on planet Earth! We will study this in more detail later, so stay tuned! The best is yet to come!!!

The fifth term for hell is a Greek phrase **The Lake of Fire.** This is the phrase used in the Bible to describe the final judgments of God. The Lake of Fire is depicted as burning with sulfur and brimstone. In the **LXX** Septuagint, the Greek word **Theion** is used to describe flashing brimstone of sulfur used to fumigate and purify. The root word of Theion is a Greek word that refers to God as divine and supreme. This goes along with the Biblical verses that state our **God is a consuming fire**! In the Bible, the throne room of God is depicted as a lake of fire that is holy, pure and depicts the presence of God. **The Fire of God** is carried in the power of the Holy Spirit and is a big part of our lives both now and in the future. The trials and fires of this life can purify us or destroy us now, just as the **Great White Throne** judgment of **Revelation 20** can purify or destroy us! Fire is a symbol of God's presence and is also a symbol of purification and judgment in the Bible. The Spirit of Burning is God's fire that has the power to change us or destroy us.

This brings us to what it means to go to Hell or the Lake of Fire! Is Hell an eternal barbeque pit or is it the presence of God? I believe the references we have studied conclude that the Lake of Fire is God's Throne Room! This is a great mystery and yet a truth that has been believed by many of God's people. Of course, there is great mystery as to what happens when a person dies. Throughout the history of the Bible there have been different interpretations and beliefs about the afterlife and what happens when people die. **The Old Testament and Hebrew writers and theologians did not all agree and neither do New Testament Christians.** So who or what are we to believe? I think we have to study the Bible ourselves and realize that not everyone is going to agree on this heated topic! However, that does not mean we can't discover truth and understand the Bible.

The first step in understanding the doctrine of Hell is to understand **the character of God.** Is God mad as Hell! Is He going to torture people in a barbeque pit forever and forever? Would God send someone to Hell if they never heard the Gospel or understood the Gospel? What if people were mislead and did not understand? Is God just going to say "Tough luck, go to hell!" Is God this unfair and unjust? Is God the God of a second chance? Where does it say that after we die there is no opportunity to embrace the love of God and enter into eternity?

If **God is Love** and He instructs us to love our enemies, would He contradict Himself by hating those He created? In **1 Corinthians 13,** the Bible states that love is patient, kind, not jealous, not pompous, not inflated, not rude, not selfish or self serving, not easily angered, does not brood over wrong doings but rejoices in the truth! Love bears all things, believes in people, always has hope, and endures all things. Love never fails! The greatest attribute of God is love and the Bible encourages us to pursue God's love and enact love in all we say and do.

Therefore, we should expect the same with God. God is not an angry, mean, masochist who wants to torture and kill people in a barbeque pit! Why would we believe that our Daddy would do such a horrific thing to his children? In fact, in the Old Testament, God said he hated this kind of thing in **Jeremiah 7:30-31** when people were offering children to be burned on idolatrous alters in the **Valley of Ben-hinnom.** This act was condemned by God and he made it clear that it would never enter His mind to do such a thing! So when Jesus used this valley as an example of punishment in the Gospels, he would not have been promoting a **hellish** doctrine of burning people! God made it clear in the writings of Jeremiah that he did not approve of such a thing! God is not an Adolph Hitler who puts His enemies in concentration camps to gas them and burn them because they reject Him. **God is love!** According to the Bible, God demonstrated His love for us all in that while we were all sinners, Christ died for us! Therefore, **The Lake of Fire** is wonderful place where God's love and justice can be ministered.

In summarization, I believe that this bible study honors the scriptures but more importantly, it honors God and His character. God is not an angry, upset, masochist who is out to send everybody to an eternal torture chamber of fire. God is not a monster who kills, steals and destroys. **GOD is LOVE!** For God so loved the world He gave His only begotten Son. God desires for all to be saved and come into the knowledge of the truth. He is the God of a second and third chance. He will forgive 70 times 7 a day. God is not out to get you with His wrath. He is out to get you, but it is with love, not condemnation. Yes, we have a choice. Yes, we are responsible for our actions. What we sow is what we reap. That is God's judgment. He warns us and we pay the price for our actions good or bad. However, in the end, I believe everyone will be given a chance to respond to God's love.

Through all this we see a picture of a new heaven and a new earth with a new order. The earth and the cosmos are being renewed, restored and reestablished on earth as it is in heaven. The visible and invisible creation of God's Cosmos will cross over into a new creation. Time and existence as we know it will end by being set free by the passion and emotion of God's love. God's Spirit will sweep across all of creation and the cosmos to consume the world with His presence. It is a divine Lake of Fire that purifies and causes people and all of creation to burn with a desire to experience God's love! All of creation will glow with God's love as God's Spirit of Fire is poured out on all flesh! In **Roman 8:18-39,** the Bible teaches us that all of creation anticipates this great day!

Chapter Nine

Conclusion

*I*T IS MY HOPE THAT this handbook has helped and assisted you to become a freethinking individual who has discovered your true potential in life. I believe everyone deserves to live a life filled with love, joy, peace, goodness, and beauty. So many people drift through life and miss out on their full potential! My prayer for you is affirming you to be all that you can be! I hope that you will succeed in every area of your life and that you will live life to ITS fullest extent. IT is your birthright and IT is your destiny if you desire for IT to be so. So go back and read this book over and over until you have fully grasped the ideas and concepts discussed. Then examine your life and open yourself up to God and the universe to expand your horizons and become the person you were created to be. I pray you will be free to be yourself and expand the character and image of God in all you do. IT is your life! Do not allow others to live IT for you! **IT is your time!**

Biographical

Dr. Stanley W. Gravely, PhD is a trained minister who over the years he has been inspired by God to serve you in your journey in life. Along with the school of hard knocks, Dr. Gravely was trained in several Bible colleges and earned two Bible diplomas, a Bachelor of Theology, a Masters and a Ph.D. in Counseling. Dr. Gravely is also a certified Human Behavior Consultant, a certified Vitalist in Natural Healing, Hallelujah Acres Health Minister and a certified Life Science Practitioner. Dr. Gravely has served God as a Pastor, church planter, Christian counselor, teacher, outreach leader, senior saint minister, youth director, musician and Deacon. He has been a Houseparent, Counselor and Program Director for a Christian children's home and an adult handicap ministry. Dr. Gravely presently is a motivation speaker, life coach, and business entrepreneur.

Dr. Gravely has been married to and assisted by his wife, Jodie, since 1979. Jodie is a musician and teacher, and presently assists people financially and physically in her own health and nutrition business. She home schooled all their children and helps others who have a desire to educate their children. The Gravely's have three children and five grandchildren.

Dr. Gravely and Jodie love people and make themselves available to all that need assistance in their journey with God. It is their sincere desire to encourage, edify, and motivate people to be successful in every area of life. You can contact Dr. Gravely or Jodie at this website, www.drstanphd.com.

Disclaimer

Dr. Gravely is not a medical doctor and is not qualified to practice medicine or trained to diagnose, treat or prescribe for medical ailments or disease. Persons requiring medical attention should consult a licensed medical doctor. The information presented here is for educational purposes. The ideas and concepts are given strictly for your information to do with as you please. You will assume all responsibility for what you do with this information.

CPSIA information can be obtained at www.ICGtesting.com
Printed in the USA
BVOW001544090513